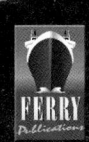

Ferry Publications Ltd
PO Box 33, Ramsey, Isle of Man, IM99 4LP
Tel: +44 (0) 1624 898445
Fax: +44 (0) 1624 898449
E-mail: FerryPubs@manx.net
Website: www.ferrypubs.co.uk

MILES COWSILL & JOHN HENDY
WITH CONTRIBUTIONS FROM JUSTIN MERRIGAN, MURRAY PATERSON, DON RIPLEY & RICHARD SEVILLE

Foreword
by Commodore John Arthur

I am very pleased to have been asked to introduce this book concerning the Sealink 'Saints'.

Having stood by during the building of the *Vortigern* in 1969 and remained in her command for eleven years, I felt sure that all the experience gained would assist me to bring out our new ship, the *St. Anselm*.

On our delivery voyage to Dover, once we had rounded Land's End and sailed into the English Channel, there was plenty of space and no shipping. Here I went through all the drills of berthing - both head first and stern first, emergency stopping, swinging and all the manoeuvring that I could think about. It all helped and on our arrival in Dover Harbour there were no problems getting in and out of the berths.

When bad weather came, the ship's power was such that assistance from a tug was never necessary. The *St. Anselm* was certainly a fine vessel to be in with my retirement coming up. This took place after thirty-six and a half years on 18th August 1981.

I am sure that all those who were connected with Sealink will enjoy this book and wish it well. Its photographic content is unrivalled and it gives an accurate account of the careers of all four 'Saints,' one of which is still happily sailing in UK waters.

*Commodore John Arthur on the bridge of the new **St. Anselm** in October 1980. (Sealink UK Ltd)*

*The **St. Anselm** passes the western pier head, with bow visor being raised in readiness for her arrival at Calais while the **St. Christopher** swings before another 90 minute dash for Dover. (Calais Chamber of Commerce)*

Building the 'Saints' by Don Ripley - former BRB Deputy Naval Architect

At the time that we started the design process of the four Saint-class ferries, the upper management of Sealink did not envisage that many of the ports that we used could sustain the cost of new terminals to give two level loading for vehicles, neither did they consider that the terminals at the outer ends of the routes could sustain those costs either.

You must remember that the transition from one to two level loading was a very big step to take. Costs of new terminals were high, bearing in mind that for each generation of bigger and heavier ships the quay walls and buttressing had to be strengthened. Some of the older quay walls had been built in the late 1800s when ships were much smaller, and there was little emphasis on fast turnaround times. Where the end of the ferry fitted into the 'shoe' of piling to give precise location to the ship to accept the linkspan and protect the shore bridge from damage, the strength of the quay was vital to accept the heavier impact loads of larger ships berthing in rough weather. The height above water of mooring decks, and consequently height in relation to the quay meant that shore attachments needed to be made higher to give an acceptable angle of mooring wires.

The most important factor though, in most places where two level loading was being considered was space. A single level shore bridge could be, and was accessed directly from the normal vehicle parking area, but an upper level linkspan had to rise, at a declivity of perhaps

Harland & Wolff's yard at Belfast with the **St. Christopher** *(left) and* **St. Anselm** *fitting out during 1980. (Robert Anderson)*

not more than one in eight, about six metres above the lower bridge, have a separate approach road, and a much higher and stronger tower structure to house the raising and lowering machinery. Do not forget either, the large rises and falls of tide levels, and therefore the end of the ship in relation to the quay platforms. In the Baltic, with only about one metre rise and fall in tides, the operations can be carried out with very much shorter linkspans, in many cases no more than six or eight metres. With a rise and fall of tide in Jersey and St Malo of about twelve metres, the length of the shore bridge is massive and needs to be supported on pontoons which can be ballasted up or down or on the tower structure.

The other factor which has even greater impact on space in the

The Saints go marching on

*The **St. Christopher** viewed from the bridge of her sister and showing the twin vehicle decks and after superstructure under construction. (Robert Anderson)*

port is the simple doubling of the vehicle loading area for each ship carrying two levels of cars/lorries and the twin effect of doubling the parking area, both for vehicles waiting for outward loading and those waiting to pass Customs and Immigration on their way in. Those who remember what the Eastern Docks Terminal at Dover looked like when the *Lord Warden* and *Maid of Kent* were the major vehicle carriers will have seen what the present volumes of traffic have necessitated in reclaimed land, massive harbour civil engineering work and buildings necessary to the rapid flow of traffic in and out. In places like Calais, where there were large areas of unoccupied land, the impact on the town itself was minimal, especially as the traffic was easily routed east and north away from the town centre, but for UK ports there were lengthy consultation and planning procedures to be completed before the ship to shore facilities could be put in place. It was also more difficult where Sealink did not own the port, as in the case of Dover.

On top of this was the finance needed to improve/replace shore facilities, both for Sealink, working under the umbrella of British Rail financial constraints, and individual ports needing to base the return of heavy investments upon the increases in tonnage and port dues from larger ships and higher number of vehicles.

The senior management in Sealink, having to take into consideration all the above points, had to suffer the ups and mainly downs of British Rail finance, tied as that was to the cycle of national economy boom and bust and also menaced every few years by the prospect of a Channel Tunnel, thought that the move from one to two level loading would be a very gradual process. That was the major reason for the new design to have the capability to load or discharge a full ship at one or both levels. It was accepted that on some routes this would be the norm for some years. In the event, the progress was

BUILDING THE 'SAINTS'

rapid, and the great advance in design was hardly ever used as intended.

The ships had to be capable of being loaded at both ro-ro decks directly from a double level shore bridge with bow and stern access. A request was made that the majority of vehicles should be able to be driven directly into their travelling positions with no manoeuvring.

I also had the requirement, which was onerous in view of the last request, that the ship should be able to load and discharge a full load of vehicles at a single level shore bridge.

To enable vehicles to transfer from one deck to another within the ship, whether it be upwards or downwards, there are two options: ramps or lifts. I examined various combinations of lifts but none was speedy enough to meet the discharge/loading target of 75 minutes. In the event I witnessed a full load of vehicles being discharged in Dover in 14 minutes, a time which was improved on later.

Proposals for ramps were drawn out time and time again but with an optimum slope for rapid transit of heavy lorries of not more than 1 in 8 and vertical transfer of about 6 metres between decks, it was impossible in the length of ship available to have single direction ramps in association with two horizontal and parallel decks.

I then doodled about with ideas to shorten the ramps and evolved the solution seen first in the *Galloway Princess* and since used on many other ro-ro carriers.

It was simple when drawn out. Lower the midships hinge point of back-to-back ramps and raise the contact point with the deck below. After a few attempts with different slopes, lengths and positions of ramps, I was able to draw out proposals for the series of ramps which were eventually fitted, and these proposals met two very important criteria for the ship. Every vehicle could be driven directly into the travelling position and this could be done, using the internal ramps, from a single or double level shore bridge.

Great scepticism was levelled at the earlier proposals, but it soon became apparent that a great solution had been evolved. This was borne out by the adoption of similar solutions on many later ro-ro carriers.

GALLOWAY PRINCESS, ST. ANSELM, ST. CHRISTOPHER

With the less onerous passage times of the Stranraer - Larne route and the relatively longer sea passages, the port and commercial managers for the route considered that a permanent factor of saving fuel on passage had to take precedence over a bow rudder which would save a few minutes in manoeuvring in port. The Dover service

Dover's first 'Saint' proudly shows off her name in the yard while ladders and cables drape across her superstructure. (Robert Anderson)

The Saints go marching on

*The **St. Christopher** in dry dock at Chatham in January 1985 showing the extension to her after accommodation which was added at Belfast two years previously. (John Hendy)*

was a quite different story. Research on earlier ships had highlighted that five minutes saved in turnround time meant one knot less speed required between Dover and Calais and the use of a bow rudder would have considerable effect on speedy manoeuvring in port. As mentioned when speaking about the trials of the three later ships, the larger bow thrusters would have an even greater impact on harbour times but we did not know that until the sea trials.

LIFESAVING APPLIANCES

The arrangement of lifesaving appliances was always the subject of deep and lengthy discussions between the design team, the Marine Superintendents, and the ships' crews. Sealink were into the use of marine escape systems, MES, using inflatable liferafts entered from deployed inflatable chutes as a major means of escape. We had fitted davit-launched liferafts for many years and the arrangement of these fitted very well into the disposition of lifeboats along each side of the ship. The LSA length was increasingly important to ferry designers, as numbers of passengers increased far more in proportion to the space available for boats and rafts. That was one major reason, years ago, to fit inflatable rafts in lieu of a full complement of rigid boats. The capacity of lifeboats had also been reduced over the years, partly because of the re-measurement, partly to comply with modern IMO requirements for enclosed or partially enclosed craft to replace open boats.

With high-sided ferries, the length taken by marine escape systems could not be integrated into a normal outfit of boats and rafts when embarkation was at a high level. The deployment of the chutes along a ship's side precludes the lowering of boats in that area. There was an alternative proposed by Dunlop many years ago using chutes at right angles to the ship, but again, much space would have been lost by

BUILDING THE 'SAINTS'

*During the ownership of Sea Containers, modifications to the ships' interiors were carried out. The **St. Anselm's** open-plan restaurant greatly benefitted. (Sealink British Ferries)*

*One of the **St. Anselm's** comfortable side lounges. (Sealink British Ferries)*

positioning guy ropes to hold the chute in position. It was only when we came to the conversions of the *Fantasia* and *Fiesta* that we were able to arrange embarkation into the chutes from sponson level that the MES became a practicality, with the entry being much closer to sea level and with a correspondingly shorter chute.

Certainly, on the four Saints there was not enough length to accommodate the required number of lifeboats plus MES. You must also remember that with higher numbers of rafts, higher numbers of lifeboats are required by international regulation to manoeuvre the rafts away from a ship in distress.

All these points kept Sealink on the davit launched scenario.

INTERIOR DESIGN

These four ships were the last major projects for Ward Associates. They had been introduced to ship interior design, as Ward & Austin, by the British Transport Commission Design Team way back in 1958 to produce the interiors for the *Maid of Kent*, and continued right up to *St Helen* in 1983. In those twenty five years they had produced interior designs for every new ship and major conversion except for the *Caesarea* in 1960, which was done by the British Rail architects under Ray Moorcroft. Their remit was to prepare interior design work covering layout of public and service spaces, design furniture to suit particular routes and purposes, produce colour schemes for each space, together with selecting materials for both soft and hard furnishings.

The Saints go marching on

They also produced constructional details for panelling, ceilings, built-in furniture, service counters, and lighting fittings. An important part of their remit was to carry out similar design work for the cabins for Captain and Chief Engineer Officer, and any passenger cabins that were required.

As a final work on the ships, Ward Associates were deeply involved in the enlargement of the duty-free shopping precincts after the ships had been in service for a time.

CONVERSION

When the decision was taken to enlarge the duty-free shopping area on the *St. Anselm* and *St. Christopher*, we made additional space by extending the deckhouse over the open mooring deck aft. Up to that time this space had been used for commercial vehicles carrying certain categories of dangerous goods that could only be accommodated on the open deck on a passenger ship. This was high-earning capacity that we did not wish to lose and to enable Sealink to continue this traffic we extended the vehicle space drencher system to the underside of the new deckhouse, left the sides open as far as possible, fitting only sufficient structure to support the new house, and fitted Class A60 structural fire insulation to the underside of the new deckhead and to the inner side of the upper vehicle space, including the main access door. This door had to be modified from its original guillotine operation to hinge up under the new deckhead without losing deck stowage space. Design work was drawn up in conjunction with MacGregors who modified the door, fitted a whole new sealing arrangement, and adapted the hydraulic gear to suit the new arrangement.

The upper Tea Bar areas in the Dover twins were alternatives to the main restaurants and underwent a number of modifications during the ships' careers. (Sealink UK Ltd)

*The bridge of the **Stena Caledonia** photographed while she was alongside at Stranraer in September 2000. (John Hendy)*

THE DOVER 'SAINTS'
by John Hendy

Initial ideas for what were to become the Sealink 'Saint' class quartet of ferries, were first drawn up during the mid-1970s at a time when cross-Channel hovercraft were threatening the status-quo. Both foot passengers and tourist car traffic were greatly attracted to the concept of speed across the Dover Strait and for a brief period, the hovercraft operations made hay while the sun shone.

However, hovercraft could not carry freight vehicles and rivals Townsend and British Rail realised that future profits lay in this greatly expanding market.

Following the immediate success of the *Galloway Princess* on the North Channel, the second and third of the series were destined for Sealink's Dover – Calais service.

The 22 mile link was and remains the most competitive of all cross-Channel services and the twin Sealink ships were very much required as a positive response to the trio of new 23 knot, double-deck, drive-through vessels which rivals Townsend Thoresen had ordered at Bremerhaven. With entry into service during 1980, the new ships were capable of making the crossing in under an hour.

NEW GENERATION

The year 1980 therefore was Sealink's opportunity to compete with their rivals or a more or less equal footing. Sealink partners SNCF Armement Naval had also ordered a new ship and so six purpose-built vessels on the most intensive route of all promised

The **St. Christopher**, viewed from the end of the Eastern Arm, powers into Dover Harbour in June 1981. (John Hendy)

some exciting times ahead.

Since the early days of transporting vehicles across the channel in specially adapted or constructed ships, much had occurred in terms of ship design, the nature and volume of the traffic and the method by which it was loaded/ unloaded.

Lift on –lift off gave way to drive on – drive off at the stern and then drive-through. The latter method, pioneered in the UK by Thoresen at Southampton in 1964, saved time and greatly contributed towards a slicker, more intensive service. Both British Rail and partners SNCF converted the *Chantilly* followed by the half-sisters *Holyhead Ferry I* and *Dover* (each now capable of carrying 26 commercial vehicles and renamed *Earl Leofric* and *Earl Siward*) to

*A new **St. Anselm** viewed on passage to Calais and showing the original sky-walk which allowed foot passengers to walk on and off at Dover. (Sealink UK Ltd)*

THE DOVER 'SAINTS'

drive-through status allowing for the carriage of more freight on their vehicle decks.

Sealink's new generation of ferries were to provide two complete drive-through freight decks with a mezzanine deck for cars between, the 'Saints' giving capacity for 62 x 12 metre lorries (up to 4.42 metres high) or 309 cars. As such they represented a completely new era in cross-Channel ship design.

DIFFERENCES

There were of course significant differences between Townsend's *Spirit of Free Enterprise* class of three ships and the Sealink 'Saints' and at the time they attracted much interest and discussion in the shipping press.

The use of twin inboard turning screws to drive the 'Saints' continued Sealink's belief that manoeuvrability was enhanced by each propeller acting on a spade rudder. Townsend believed that the triple screw arrangement gave the best straight-line manoeuvres in high crosswind conditions. It also allowed for maintenance on one engine to be carried out whilst the ship was kept in service using the other two.

Lifesaving equipment was also to be different between the rival classes of ship. Whereas Townsend Thoresen employed the new aircraft-type passenger chutes, Sealink opted for the more traditional arrangement with six glass-fibre diesel-driven lifeboats and 20 inflatable lifeboats.

As the shipping arm of the British Railways Board and a nationalised company, Sealink's role was clearly defined and was simply to transport all types of traffic that needed to travel. Townsend Thoresen on the other hand had no such constraints eg their ships would never be inundated with trains full of rail-connected passengers and their luggage. They could therefore be designed in a completely different manner with a greater emphasis on motorists, day-trippers or lorry drivers.

SAINTS

There were not just differences between the Dover 'Saints' and their German-built competitors but also between the other two of the Belfast-built Sealink 'Saint' class. They were all built to the same principal dimensions but the 'Galloway's' wheelhouse was a deck lower while the final ship, *St. David*, had an after wheelhouse fitted to

The addition of the Sun Deck on Bridge Deck level made a tremendous difference to the Dover twins and gave excellent all-round views of the Channel. (John Hendy)

The Saints go marching on

aid stern-first navigation on the Holyhead – Dun Laoghaire route.

Whereas the *Galloway Princess* was fitted with three Allen-powered alternators (common in most recently-built Sealink ships at that time), the other three vessels were given three Harland & Wolff – M.A.N. diesel-driven alternators. The reason for this was that the licence agreement between Harland & Wolff and M.A.N. was not concluded until 1977 when the equipment for the first ship had already been decided.

Another significant difference was the use of a bulbous bow rather than a bow rudder in the *Galloway Princess*. Apart from short periods of docking, the 'Galloway' was not required to navigate stern first and so a bulbous bow of the Vickers St Albans type was fitted.

In the best Dover railway-vessel tradition, both 'Saints' were fitted with bow-rudders. To cope with the expected high crosswinds likely to be encountered at both Dover and Calais, they were also fitted with two 1,000 kW KaMeWa bow thrusters which developed a 20 tonne thrust. They were found to be effective when going astern at speeds up to 10 knots and the twin ships proved to be the most manoeuvrable ferries using either port. In time, inclement weather conditions would send tugs rushing to the aid of all others but the Sealink 'Saints' were able to cope with almost everything that the Dover Strait threw at them.

Passenger comfort was also aided by twin Denny Brown AEG stabilizers each having an area of 6.04 m2.

Cross-sectional drawings of the ships show the quite pronounced 1:26 slope on the main vehicle decks (Decks B and D) towards amidships. This key aspect of their design served to keep the vehicle decks as low as possible but did apparently cause some problems for the installation of the main engines as the vehicle decks reached their lowest points immediately above the main engine spaces.

From the outset, Sealink had always seen a time when the Dover 'Saints' might be moved elsewhere and so another important feature in their construction was the fitting of four MacGregor hydraulic ramps each capable of being raised with up to six lorries weighing 150 tons on it. The ramps measured approximately 36.4 metres long by 6.7 metres wide and were locked in the upper position to form the greater part of B Deck.

While both Dover and Calais were both fitted with two-tier ramps, very few other ports serving Sealink ships could at that time

Following the addition of extra accommodation at their after ends, the Dover 'Saints' had their passenger certificates increased to 1,400. (John Hendy)

13

THE DOVER 'SAINTS'

claim such advancement in port infrastructure hence the importance of raising vehicles to the upper deck via internal ramps. Rather optimistically, Sealink announced that all future new-buildings should not require internal ramps: as we now know, there were no future new-buildings as Sealink was denationalised in 1984.

MacGregor also supplied the vessels' stern doors which were constructed in two sections. When raised, the bow visor gave an opening to D Deck of 6.7 metres and a 5 metre headroom for vehicles entering the upper level (B Deck). Inside the weatherproof visor was the MacGregor watertight door. Protecting B Deck were two guillotine doors, one aft and one forward beneath the superstructure.

Townsend Thoresen had opted for the 'Neat Stow' clam door for their 'Spirit' class. Rather than swinging out and up as did the visor, the 'Neat Stow' doors slid alongside the bow opening. The manner in which these doors were operated led to the tragic capsize of the *Herald of Free Enterprise* (the second of the trio), seven years later.

ENGINE ROOM

The engine rooms were divided into three water-tight compartments the after space containing the main engines in the form of two Crossley-Pielstick 16PC2V Mk.5 unidirectional diesel engines driving inward-turning controllable pitch propellers. In the choice of the Mk. 5 engine was another modification of the 'Galloway' design. The Mk. 5 allowed for the greater power required to produce a 19.5 knot service speed – one knot faster than the *Galloway Princess* which was fitted with Mk. 2 engines: 8,000 bhp at 507 rev/min as opposed to 10,400 bhp at 520 rev/min.

With world oil prices rising and very much to an eye on

*Much has happened at Calais since this photograph was taken in 1980 as the **St. Anselm** creeps up to her berth adjacent to the Gare Maritime. (FotoFlite)*

The Saints go marching on

*Together in their home port at last on 14th April 1981. The **St. Anselm** leaves on her afternoon Calais sailing while the newly arrived **St. Christopher** lays-by at the end of the Eastern Arm. (John Hendy)*

economy, Sealink announced that the new Dover ships would burn 6.2 tonnes of fuel per round trip. Townsend Thoresen refused to disclose its figures but Sealink officials believed their fuel costs were 25% greater making a 'Spirit' class vessel burn 7.75 tonnes of fuel on a return sailing. The speed of the 'Spirit' class enabled them to operate five round sailings a day (burning 38.75 tonnes) whereas the Sealink ships only managed four sailings (24.8 tonnes)..

INSIDE

Designed by British Rail's London-based interior design consultant Ward Associates, the main accommodation for the 1,000 passengers originally carried was on A Deck (Boat Deck).

In this writer's view, it was far from successful being of an open-plan nature and therefore tending to be crowded and noisy during busy passages. With the food mall in the centre of the accommodation, the area was frequently full of queues, smells and dirty plates.

This was hardly surprising as the original concept for the ships was to carry in the region of 600 passengers, it being felt at the time that hovercraft developments in the form of the two stretched SRN 4s and the twin SNCF 'naviplanes' would soon see the majority of passengers opting for speed rather than comfort. Both Townsend and British Rail were concerned by this trend and figures showed that in the peak month of August 1977 hovercraft had carried 24% of cars

THE DOVER 'SAINTS'

and 25% of passengers on the short-sea routes..

The Italian company Cantrisa manufactured and supplied many items although Harland & Wolff actually completed the out fitting.

On the Promenade Deck above, the tea bar and lounge catered for 98 people and was furnished with yellow tables and green seats and benches.

On the Boat Deck, the bar had room for 214 passengers and was originally a red and purple colour combination with a mixture of bench-type sofas and separate armchairs. A recess for gaming machines and a casino led off from this area. The after lounge accommodated 155 people and was decorated in blues and greens with off-white seats. Off this lounge and also the midships lounge were the side lounges fitted with aircraft-type seats. The midship lounge and griddle provided room for 286 people divided off by glass partitions. A serve-yourself three-course meal was available for about £1.82 in 1980!

The drivers' lounge was also situated on the Boat Deck and catered for 48 passengers, offering them a bar and lounge area with just five tables for eating (full breakfast was available for £1), a television, coffee maker and toilet.

In addition there was a passport office, a first-aid room, a bank and a nursing mothers' toilet which was something of an innovation at that time. Cabins were provided for 30 passengers in two-birth cabins on A and B Decks.

A new departure for BR ferries was the installation of ICL computers that monitored the cash registers on board. This duly supplied the Purser with information so that he was able to order stores and a keep a tally of what monies had been spent on board.

The outside deck spaces, although far from ample, were in great contrast to the meagre passenger areas provided on Townsend Thoresen's 'Spirit' class.. (John Hendy)

The Saints go marching on

*The **St. Christopher** arriving at Dover Eastern Docks at the conclusion of an afternoon sailing from Calais. (Sealink British Ferries)*

FOOT PASSENGERS

The embarkation of foot passengers onto vehicle ferries has always presented problems and for many years they walked on board across the car decks.

However, the Dover 'Saints' were fitted with the now universal 'skywalk' at the stern in order that passengers could walk directly from A Deck ashore via their own footbridge. At Calais, the ships berthed bow-in with port-sides adjacent to the Gare Maritime where day-trippers were collected from the quay side by buses.

The Townsend 'Spirit' class tended not to use these berths and docked at the newer linkspans. The first of the larger berths in the outer part of the harbour, berth 5, was constructed to coincide with the appearance of the *Spirit of Free Enterprise* in 1980.

The Sealink 'Saints' were not initially involved in any of the train-connected services at Calais Maritime. It would have been totally inconceivable that these prestigious ships could have been delayed by hundreds of foot passengers with their heavy luggage but in any case, racks for this purpose were not fitted in either ship.

In 1980 Sealink retained the 'classic' passenger turbine steamer *Caesarea* to mop-up this trade and after she had passed to Hong Kong buyers at the end of the year, in 1981 the *Caledonian Princess* was brought in to operate the seasonal services.

As we shall see later, there eventually came a time when the "Saints" were used on a Dover Western Docks – Calais train-connected service after which chaos ensued.

RETROSPECT

Such was the pace of change that within six years of entering service the Dover

THE DOVER 'SAINTS'

*This view shows the two different designs of vessels built for the short-sea services during the early '80s. The **St. David** can be seen at Calais' berth 3 while at berth 2 is the ill-fated **Herald of Free Enterprise**. (Miles Cowsill)*

'Saints' were seen as too small following Townsend Thoresen's (later P&O European Ferries) introduction of their successful 'Chunnel Beaters' the *Pride of Dover* and *Pride of Calais*.

Plans to stretch the 'Saints' to compete with the larger ships were abandoned as Sea Containers (who had purchased Sealink in 1984) introduced converted twin deep-sea ro-ro vessels in the form of the *Fantasia* and *Fiesta*.

After Stena Line had assumed control of Sealink in 1990, both 'Saints' were moved to the Irish Sea thereby joining their half sisters but the introduction of the huge loss-making HSS 1500 catamarans from 1996 was the seal their fates on both the Holyhead – Dun Laoghaire and Stranraer – Belfast routes.

Both 'Saints' completed their UK service on the Newhaven – Dieppe link which continued to lose money and was finally closed with the withdrawal of the *Stena Cambria* in January 1999.

GALLOWAY PRINCESS/STENA GALLOWAY by Miles Cowsill

In the light of further increases in traffic between Northern Ireland and the UK and increased competition from Townsend Thoresen at Cairnryan, it was announced in Autumn 1977 that a new purpose-built ship for the Stranraer-Larne service would be ordered from Harland & Wolff for delivery in Spring 1979. The new vessel would be designed as a double-deck drive on - drive off ferry with a capacity to carry 300 cars and 600 passengers. Prior to the introduction of the new ship, new twin-level berths had to be constructed at both Stranraer and Larne. The design of this ship with her other three sisters was the culmination of nearly five years' design work.

During the construction of the *Galloway Princess* her passenger capacity was increased from 600 to 1,000.

Compared to her later near sisters, the 'Galloway' had less accommodation as it was envisaged there would not be the traffic in the long-term for the route.

When the 'Galloway' was ordered, services on the North Channel were in the hands of the *Antrim Princess*, *Ailsa Princess* and later the *Darnia*; it was planned that on the arrival of the new vessel that the 'Antrim' would be transferred within the fleet.

1979

The *Galloway Princess* was launched at Harland & Wolff without ceremony on the morning of 24th May. At this time it was planned that she would enter service in October.

*The **Galloway Princess** was launched at Harland & Wolff on 24th May 1979. (Hamish Ross collection)*

1980

Following her fitting out, delays at Harland & Wolff meant that the *Galloway Princess* did not enter service until 1st May on the 08.30 sailing from Stranraer to Larne. After only a few weeks in service she experienced mechanical problems and had to be withdrawn from service for a week at the end of June.

1982

The 'Galloway's' operating partner, the *Ailsa Princess* was transferred from Stranraer for a new career on the Weymouth-Cherbourg service and later renamed *Earl Harold*. Meanwhile, the freight vessel *Darnia* underwent extension work to her passenger

*This view shows the **Galloway Princess** shortly after her launch being manoeuvred by tugs to her fitting-out berth. (Hamish Ross collection)*

The Saints go marching on

The Galloway Princess arrives off the port of Larne during her first season in operation. (Harry Cathcart)

accommodation thereby enabling her to fulfil a multi-purpose role alongside alongside the *Galloway Princess* and *Antrim Princess*.

1983

Following a serious engine room fire on board the *Antrim Princess* on 9th December 1982, the fourth vessel in the quartet of ships the *St David* was sent from Holyhead to take her place. This was the first time that the 'Galloway' and *St David* were to operate on the same route.

1984

The *Galloway Princess*, like her other operating partners in the Sealink fleet, appeared without the BR double arrow logo on her funnels in readiness for privatisation of Sealink UK Limited.

1985

The *Antrim Princess* left Stranraer for a new role in the company on the Heysham-Douglas route. Her place was taken by the larger *St. David* from Holyhead in Spring 1986.

1989

During the overhaul of the *Galloway Princess* she was relieved by the ALA French train ferry *Saint Eloi*, which proved to be a totally

From left to right: H&W representative, Fergus Gibson, General Manager, Sealink Scotland, Tony Rogan, Chief Naval Architect, Sealink U.K, Bert Cockett, Sealink U.K, Steve Dickman, New Building Superintendent, Sealink U.K, Captain & Marine Supt. Hamish Ross, Shipping and Port Manager Sealink Scotland. (Hamish Ross collection)

GALLOWAY PRINCESS/STENA GALLOWAY

*The **Darnia** and the **Galloway Princess** alongside at Stranraer on 30th April 1980. The 'Galloway' had just arrived back from a VIP visit to Glasgow. (Tom Hamilton)*

unsuitable vessel for the route in her absence.

1990

Following a fire on board the *St. Columba* at Holyhead, the now redundant *Earl Granville* was sent to Stranraer to operate alongside the 'Galloway', which in turn allowed the *St. David* to be sent south to cover for the 'Columba's' absence. Again the 'Granville' proved to be totally unsuitable for the route and in the end had to operate alongside the train ferry *Cambridge Ferry* in order to maintain freight carryings during the period.

During 1990, Sea Containers, which had acquired Sealink in 1984, sold its ferry operations to Stena Line of Sweden. Following the reorganisation of the company it was announced that all vessels would be renamed allowing for the prefix 'Stena' to be added to all vessel names in the fleet. As a result of this, the 'Galloway' was renamed *Stena Galloway* and appeared in the modified livery of Sealink Stena Line.

At the end of the year it was announced that the *St. Christopher* would be transferred from Dover and renamed *Stena Antrim* for her new role at Stranraer. With the arrival of the 'Antrim', this saw three of the 'Saint' class vessels operating together on the route, something which had never been envisaged when they were ordered by Sealink

*The **Galloway Princess** is pictured during her first week in operations on the Stranraer-Larne service following her late delivery by her builders.. (Hamish Ross collection)*

GALLOWAY PRINCESS/STENA GALLOWAY

The 'Galloway' arrives off the entrance to Larne Lough in January 1984. (Ken Kane)

*The **Galloway Princess** outward bound from Larne following privatisation of the company. (Miles Cowsill)*

in 1978. It did, however, demonstrate the inter-route flexibility of the vessels' basic design.

1992

The *Stena Galloway* made her first 'away visit' from her home port in July, when the *Stena Cambria* experienced gearbox problems. On 23rd July, she made her debut on the Holyhead-Dun Laoghaire service, operating in tandem with the *Stena Hibernia*, (ex *St. Columba*) while, following a brief drydocking, the *Stena Cambria* transferred to the shorter Larne – Stranraer crossing operating on one main engine. The 'Galloway' was not the ideal vessel on the Holyhead link as she was unable to operate in drive-through mode. Due to her hull form with a bulbous bow she could not berth bow-in at the linkspans on either side of the Irish Sea and operated for the period as a stern – loading vessel in both ports. The 'Galloway' returned to her home port on 21st August. The choice of the *Stena Galloway* was a strange choice as the *Stena Caledonia* would have been a far better fit in both ports.

1993

The *Galloway Princess* appeared in the further new livery of Stena Sealink Line. In July Stena Sealink Line announced that they planned to build two massive high-speed ferries, the first of which was to be placed on the Holyhead-Dun Laoghaire route while the second was

The Saints go marching on

*The **Galloway Princess** swings off the berth at Stranraer outward-bound for Ireland. (Miles Cowsill)*

Following the take-over of Sealink by Stena Line there were two different liveries before the vessels were repainted in Stena Line livery. This view shows the 'Galloway' arriving at Larne in the last of the Sealink liveries. (Gordon Hislip)

to follow to Stranraer.

1995

At the end of the year the famous brand name 'Sealink' was relinquished in favour of the Swedish trading name of Stena Line.

Following mounting speculation for over a year, the company decided to withdraw their North Channel operations from Larne in favour of Belfast. On 12th November, the *Stena Antrim* made the last sailing from the port of Larne.

1996

On 21st July, the *Stena Voyager* (the second HSS) commenced operations between Stranraer and Larne. Operations on the route were now marketed very heavily around the HSS service, which resulted in a lower profile role for *Stena Galloway* and her operating partner, the *Stena Caledonia*.

Two months later, it was announced that the 'Galloway' would primarily operate as a freight vessel in future and would only operate as a passenger ship during the peak periods. Her passenger certificate was reduced to just 100 passengers.

1998

The *Stena Galloway* was sent to refit at Swansea, South Wales. Later in the year, the 'Galloway' had to return to full passenger operations

25

GALLOWAY PRINCESS/STENA GALLOWAY

*This interesting view shows the **Galloway Princess** inward-bound from Larne passing P&O European Ferries' **Pride of Rathlin** in Loch Ryan. (Miles Cowsill)*

following the 'Voyager' being transferred to the North Sea operations of the company. This was due to problems with the third HSS craft *Stena Discovery*.

2000

In a surprise move, Stena Line announced that they planned to move back to Larne as from September, using their conventional vessels *Stena Galloway* and *Stena Caledonia*. Each vessel would operate three round trips a day. In the event the planned move did not take place. May 1st saw the 20th anniversary of the maiden commercial voyage of the *Galloway Princess*. The *Stena Galloway* was dressed overall while lying alongside at the Stena Line terminal at Belfast on that day to mark the occasion. This was just across the River Lagan from her birthplace at Harland & Wolff.

2001

At Fishguard the *Koningin Beatrix* suffered some major engine problems during the summer period on the Rosslare service which

The Saints go marching on

meant that she had to operate at a reduced service speed. At the end of the peak season she was sent for repairs and her place was taken by the *Stena Galloway* from early September until 31st October: this only her second period away from her home port during her career in UK waters.

In late Autumn it was announced that the *Stena Galloway* would be withdrawn from the Stranraer-Belfast service as from February 2002 and as a result 92 persons would be made redundant. The vessel was to be sold by Stena Line to raise further capital to meet the heavy losses on the Irish Sea. Bo Severed, in a statement to the press following this announcement, stated, "We have reached the conclusion that we have to reduce our capacity and increase the efficiency of our Belfast-Stranraer route if we are to remain competitive today and feel confident investing for tomorrow."

In the event her sale was to be very short sighted.

2002

The *Stena Galloway* completed her last sailing between Stranraer-Belfast on 22nd February. Two days later she sailed under the Moroccan flag as the *Le Rif*.

*The **Stena Galloway** is seen during her last couple of months in service with the company at Rosslare while covering the Fishguard route. (Gordon Hislip)*

The 25 year old ship remains in service today - between Tangier and Algeciras under the ownership of International Maritime Transport Corporation (IMTC).

ST. ANSELM/STENA CAMBRIA
by John Hendy

The first of Dover's twin ferries was named after an Archbishop of Canterbury who died in 1105 and who is reputed to have crossed the Channel from Dover on his way to visit the Pope in Rome.

Remembering that the twin ships were ordered in time for the lucrative 1980 summer season, their late delivery was the cause of great annoyance from the British Railways' Board who laid the blame fairly and squarely at the doors of Harland & Wolff. The Townsend Thoresen opposition had gone to West Germany for their three new ships and all had been delivered on time thereby allowing them much positive publicity and flag-waving as all three ships broke the Dover to Calais speed record and enabled TT to market their route as the 'Blue Riband' service.

As Sealink UK Ltd. was still nationalised, severe constraints were imposed by the Government of the day. The *St. Anselm*'s maiden voyage had been scheduled for 11.30 on 1st July 1980 but she was almost four months late and therefore missed the high season.

Transferring from the *Vortigern*, the new ship's Senior Master was Captain John Arthur who received the honour of being promoted to Fleet Commodore prior to the vessel entering service.

1979

In gale conditions, the ship was named by Lady Parker (wife of British Railways' Board Chairman, Sir Peter Parker) on 4th

The *St. Anselm* arriving at Dover's Admiralty Pier after trials at Calais on Sunday 26th October 1980. (John Hendy)

December. The weather was such that the *St. Anselm* was not actually launched until the winds had abated on the following day.

1980

The *St. Anselm* left Belfast in thick fog at midday on 22nd October and had not been sailing south for very long when both radars failed. Fortunately there were five navigating officers on the bridge and the fault was soon rectified. She then ran into a force 8-9 gale with long Atlantic swells in the St. George's Channel. Rounding Land's End the gales eased and trials were carried out in the lee of Falmouth, time even being found to circumnavigate the Eddystone lighthouse.

She arrived through Dover's eastern entrance in perfect weather

*A dramatic view of the **St. Anselm** going down the ways at Harland & Wolff on 5th December 1979 after having been named by Lady Parker on the previous day. (Sealink UK Ltd)*

ST. ANSELM/STENA CAMBRIA

The main vehicle deck looking aft with the raised mezzaine deck above. (Sealink UK Ltd)

*Flagship of the Sealink fleet! The **St. Anselm** leaves the White Cliffs of Dover astern during 1981. (Sealink UK Ltd)*

on Friday 24th October, immediately taking on stores and undertaking trials before sailing to the Admiralty Pier at 17.00 to lay-by overnight.. The following day, more stores and bunkers were taken on at the Eastern Docks before trials at berths 3 and 5. At 05.45 on Sunday 26th October the ship crossed to Calais for the first time. The gales had returned as the ship tested the inner-most linkspans at Calais (numbers 3 and 4) before departing for Dover at 11.00. Ninety minutes later she arrived at the eastern entrance, crossed the bay and berthed at the Admiralty Pier's berth 2 between the ro-ro ship *Anderida* and the Belgian car ferry *Prins Philippe*. The *St. Anselm* was then open to Sealink staff and friends and local management were surprised at the great interest that the ship had generated.

The *St. Anselm*'s maiden voyage was at 07.00 on Monday 27th October allowing the turbine steamer *Earl Leofric* to stand down and retire for lay-up at Newhaven.

However, on 2nd November, the *St. Anselm*'s running partner *Earl Siward* stripped some turbine blades and so the 'Leofric' returned to service a week later. Sealink originally planned to bring in Stranraers's *Antrim Princess* until the arrival of the *St. Christopher* but the *Earl Siward* was retained, finally entering service again on 11th December. The 'Leofric' remained on service for four more days allowing the *St. Anselm* to go off service for 'minor repairs" before she returned to service with the 11.30 to Calais on 17th December.

An SNCF strike at Calais between 18th – 20th December saw all

*A purposeful-looking **St. Anselm** is viewed in the buoyed channel leaving Calais for Dover. The 'cow-catcher' (on which the Calais linkspan rested) always created an impressive bow wave. (John Hendy)*

ST. ANSELM/STENA CAMBRIA

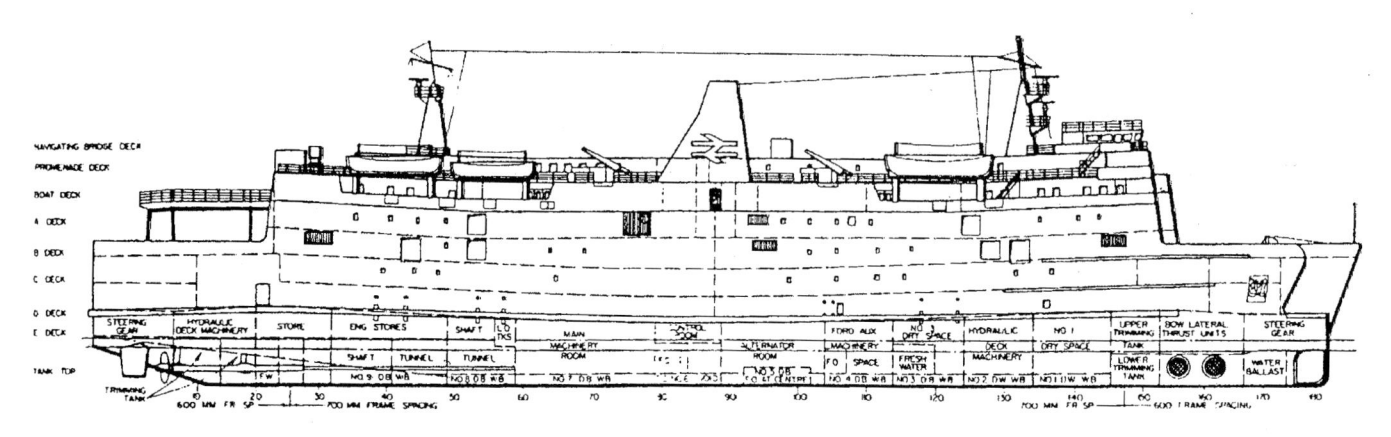

By courtesy of the The Motor Ship

local Sealink vessels sailing to Boulogne: a first visit for the new *St. Anselm*.

1981

The *Vortigern* was in service with the *St. Anselm* during January but an engine room fire in mid-month saw the *Earl Siward* recalled. Two days later she also went off service with boiler problems and so SNCF reactivated their 1958 car ferry *Compiegne* which had completed her final advertised sailings from Dover to Boulogne on 27th September. Fresh from overhaul, SNCF's *Chartres,* completed the trio of ships on the extremely imbalanced Sealink Dover – Calais service.

Gales over the weekend of 6th – 7th March saw damage to the *St. Anselm*'s 'cow-catcher.'

On 15th April, the *St. Christopher* finally took up service with the *St. Anselm* on the newly-named 'Flagship Service.' The *Chartres* remained SNCF's contribution until the arrival of the new *Cote d'Azur* which had been launched at Le Havre on 22nd December 1980.

On 1st August, local Sealink management swapped rosters between the *St. Anselm* and *St. Christopher* and also Folkestone's *Hengist* and *Horsa*.

On 18th August, Commodore John Arthur retired from service and 'B' crew Master Captain Tom Manton took over as the ship's Senior Master.

With the Belgian RMT ferry *Princesse Marie-Christine* off service

*The former **St. Christopher** is pictured as the **Ibn Batouta** outward-bound from Algeciras to Tangier. (FotoFlite)*

The *Isla de Botafoc* (ex *St. Anselm*) is pictured leaving Mahon, Minorca in August 2005. (Richard Seville)

*The former **Galloway Princess** makes a fine sight as she sails towards the Spanish coast inward bound to Algeciras as IMTC's **Le Rif**. (FotoFlite)*

An early publicity photograph of the **St. Anselm** *showing the ship prior to entering service in October 1980. (Sealink UK Ltd)*

The Saints go marching on

1983

On her return to Dover following the £750,000 modifications at Belfast, the *St. Anselm* was hastily called in to operate the Fishguard – Rosslare service vice the *Stena Normandica* operating the 14.45 to Ireland on 28th March. The *St. Anselm* arrived back in Dover on 31st March allowing the *St. Christopher* to go off for her modifications.

On 3rd June, a new four-ship service commenced between Dover and Calais following the closure of the Folkestone – Calais service. The delay of the new SNCF ship (*Champs Elysees*) saw the *Chantilly* filling the gap but unfortunately, the new schedules allowed for certain train-connected sailings to be operated from the Admiralty Pier ramp at the Western Docks.

1984

In readiness for the de-nationalisation of Sealink, ships operated throughout the season without their white BR symbols on the red funnels.

Industrial action at Calais on 25th – 26th May saw the *St. Anselm* sailing to Boulogne.

During July, the company was sold to Sea Containers for £66 million and an immediate evaluation of all ships and routes was carried out. It was mooted that the *St. Anselm* and *St. Christopher* might be switched to Folkestone – Boulogne and that larger ships would be ordered for the Dover – Calais route. The company now traded as Sealink British Ferries.

*The **St. Anselm** heads out into a msity Channel shortly after her £750,000 modification in 1983. (John Hendy)*

SNCF's new *Champs Elysees* entered service on the Calais – Dover link on 4th October.

1985

During January, the ship refitted at Smith's Ship Repairers at North Shields.

ST. ANSELM/STENA CAMBRIA

*The **St. Anselm** arriving at Calais as work progresses on the rebuilding of the port's eastern pier. (Calais Chamber of Commerce)*

Sea Containers expressed their desire to increase the 15% share then held by Sealink UK Ltd. In the Dover – Ostend service and introduced the *St. David* on the route during March causing major repercussions.

1986

During January Sealink's Belgian partners, RMT, entered into a trading agreement with Townsend Thoresen, effectively shutting both the *St. David* and Sealink British Ferries out of the Belgian port.

A new freight service linking Dover and Dunkirk West was due to commence in the New Year but manning arrangements with the recently acquired ro-ro freighter *Seafreight Freeway* saw the *St. Anselm* introduced onto the link operating the 02.30, 10.30 and 18.30 sailings from Dover Eastern Docks. The service was scheduled to operated from the Admiralty Pier berth but a strike by Townsend Thoresen meant plenty of room at the Eastern Docks. Crossing time was 2 hours 15 minutes. She was replaced by SNCF's *Transcontainer 1* during February.

As part of her new owners' policy of upratring and improving their ferries in order to remove the BR image, the *St. Anselm* was sent to Papenburg in West Germany during the early part of the year for a £1.5 million refit. The bar area now resembled a traditional English pub but the interior designers' newly-installed pink carpets in the after area were replaced after about two weeks. The duty-free shop at the after end was extended to incorporate a a gift shop and some of the windows were plated in. The Boat Deck tea bar was converted to a bistro.

With the SNCF ferry *Champs Elysees* on strike and the *Cote d'Azur* in dry dock at Dunkirk (at two days' notice), the *St. Anselm* returned to Dover prematurely with fifty German workers still on board. She

The Saints go marching on

*Going astern out of Calais in May 1985, the **St. Anselm's** bow rudder is seen at work. (John Hendy)*

recommenced service with the 11.15 on 14th March.

During October, plans were announced that Sea Containers had drawn up plans to jumboise the *St. Anselm* and *St. Christopher* by inserting an extra deck and either a 50ft or 100ft section amidships to extend them. This was in resposnse to Townsend Thoresen's announcement of two new 'Chunnel Beaters' to replace their 'Spirit' class on the Dover – Calais link.

1989

The purchase of the deep-sea ro-ro vessels which eventually became the *Fantasia* and SNCF's *Fiesta* saw initial plans for the *St. Anselm* to be switched to Fishguard and the *St. Christopher* to Newhaven.

*The **St. Anselm** makes a fine sight as she leaves the English coast astern and heads for Calais. (FotoFlite)*

55

ST. ANSELM/STENA CAMBRIA

*In what was seen as something of an act of faith by the local Sealink management, during 1990, the **St. Anselm** was switched to the Folkestone - Boulogne route (vice the **Horsa**). Traffic figures showed a healthy increase. Here is the ship arriving at the French port in 16th April 1990. (John Hendy)*

1990

In readiness for the imminent arrival of the *Fantasia*, on 11th February, the *St. Anselm* became the largest-ever ferry to serve the Folkestone – Boulogne route when was switched to operate with the *Hengist* while the *Horsa* was transferred to Holyhead.

During her refit, an Orient Express Lounge was created in her Motorists' Lounge. Trials took place at both Folkestone and Boulogne on 10th February, the first crossing being the 13.30 ex Folkestone on the following day although a mechanical problem saw her leave 27 minutes late on 1.5 engines. Bad weather later in the day saw her divert to Dover on her return trip.

With the *Fantasia* requiring a quick return to Bremerhaven for attention to a bow-thrust unit, the *St. Anselm* was returned to the Dover – Calais service from 6th – 12th June. The *Earl William* deputised at Folkestone during this period.

In a hostile take-over bid, Sealink came under the control of Stena Line of Gothenburg, Sweden who paid an inflated £259 million for the company during April. The company was restyled Sealink Stena Line and a re-evaluation of all ships and ports was immediately ordered.

On passage between Boulogne and Folkestone with the 01.45 on 19th September, a fire caused by a short-circuit in the starboard alternator caused all electrical power to be lost and the ship drifted up Channel in force 7 gusts. The port engine was restarted at 06.00 and the ship eventually berthed at Dover Eastern Docks. The *St. Anselm* therefore completed service at Folkestone rather prematurely and was sent to A&P Appledore at Wallsend for repairs.

The ship then arrived at Fishguard from overhaul on 17th November and took up

*The **St. Anselm** arriving through the eastern entrance of Dover Harbour on 29th May 1987. (John Hendy)*

ST. ANSELM/STENA CAMBRIA

*The **Stena Cambria** bow-in at Calais when running in tandem with the ro-pax **Stena Challenger** during 1994. (John Hendy)*

the Rosslare workings of the *Felicity* at 15.00 on the following day. High winds and rough seas prevented her from docking at Fishguard at 01.00 on 8th December. The ship sought shelter in Cardigan Bay before running to Swansea to discharge. She arrived there at 20.20 after which she sailed directly to Dover.

With the *Fantasia* having gone off service with a jammed bow-visor on 2nd December, the former *St. Anselm* – now renamed *Stena Cambria* – replaced her until 28th December.

1991

Following a disastrous first year's trading, Stena launched 'Operation Benchmark' to restructure and economise right across the former Sealink fleet. The *Stena Horsa* closed the 148 year old Folkestone – Boulogne link on 31st January. The restructuring saw the former *St. Anselm* switched to the Holyhead – Dun Laoghaire link to support to *St. Columba (Stena Hibernia)*..

The *Stena Cambria* was relieved at refit by the *Stena Hengist*, on one of her final duties before sailing to Stranraer to cover refits and being sold.

With the *St. Columba* away on a £7 million refit, on 11th February the *Stena Cambria* holed herself in the inner harbour at Holyhead and was sent to Birkenhead for repairs until 19th February. She was briefly replaced by the *Stena Horsa* which was followed by the *Earl William*. The *Stena Hibernia* (ex *St. Columba*) was back in service on 14th March, allowing the *Stena Cambria* to sail to Stranraer to cover refits.

With the impending arrival of the *Stena Invicta* (ex *Peder Paars*) at Dover, the *Stena Cambria* was required to deputise, replacing sister ship *Stena Antrim* from 4th April. A series of strikes at Calais saw all berths blocked on 20th June necessitating a switch to Boulogne for the *Stena Cambria*. She was initially due to return to Holyhead on 24th June after which the ro-pax freighter *Stena Challenger* should have taken her place but with so much traffic being lost to rivals P&O European Ferries, it was decided to retain her until her return to Holyhead at 18.00 on 8th July. She took up service with the 04.00 (delayed to 04.50) to Dun Laoghaire three days later. Her crossings were reduced to one a day from 1st October.

1992

The *Stena Cambria* arrived at Holyhead from overhaul at Birkenhead on 23rd January taking over the *Stena Hibernia's* roster the following day. During her absence the *Stena Hengist* provided back up after which she sailed to Stranraer to cover the port's overhaul period.

On 28th July, the *Stena Cambria* commenced operations using the new deep water, outer harbour, east berth at Holyhead and promptly suffered major gearbox problems necessitating the switch of the *Stena Galloway* (ex *Galloway Princess*) from Stranraer to replace her.

Following minor repairs Birkenhead for two days, the *Stena Cambria* was sent to the North Channel to operate the Stranraer – Larne route in a freight role and at greatly reduced speed.. Then in mid-August she was sent to major repairs at Birkenhead and finally returned to Holyhead on 21st August.

During November the *Stena Cambria* deputised at Fishguard for the *Stena Felicity* during which time her former 'Flagship Service' running partner *Chartres* took up freight sailings at Holyhead.

The same month, the company was renamed Stena Sealink Line.

1993

The *Stena Cambria* arrived for refit on 7th January but a small fire delayed her return to service.

During late May, the ship took part in the Battle of the Atlantic Fleet Review off Anglesey.

1994

During the spring, the *Stena Cambria* again returned to Dover to cover for the overhaul period of the local Sealink Stena Line fleet. She was replaced by the chartered Faeroese ferry *Noronna* at Holyhead on 26th January. With P&O European Ferries now operating a five-ship service on the Dover-Calais link, on 14th March the freighter *Stena Challenger* was switched from the Dunkirk West route to run in tandem in order to offer additional freight capacity. The *Stena Cambria* was back at Holyhead on 28th March.

1995

On 12th July, it was announced that the operational partnership between Stena Sealink Line and French partners SNAT would terminate as from 31st December. Sealink Stena announced that it would bring, "its full weight to bear on the key Continental tourist and freight short-sea sector to create an international service organisation capable of challenging any other operator." Stena would drop the name Sealink whilst the French would in future operate as SeaFrance.

The Stena Cambria arriving at Holyhead under the command Captain Tudor James. (Gordon Hislip)

ST. ANSELM/STENA CAMBRIA

*The **Stena Cambria** arrives at Dun Laoghaire on her early morning sailing from Holyhead as the **Stena Hibernia** swings in the port outward-bound for Wales. (Miles Cowsill)*

Without each other on which to rely, both operators would need to enlarge their respective fleets. Sealink Stena had provided the *Stena Fantasia*, *Stena Invicta* and the ro-pax *Stena Challenger* whilst SNAT had supplied the *Fiesta* and *Cote d'Azur*. They were soon assisted by the former train ferry *Nord Pas-de-Calais* which closed the Dunkirk West train ferry service on 22nd December thereafter operating as a ro-ro vessel on the Calais – Dover link. They also brought in the former *Stena Londoner* (renamed *SeaFrance Monet*) from the Dieppe – Newhaven service. Stena meanwhile introduced the fast craft *Stena Lynx II* which was replaced by the new *Stena Lynx III* in July 1996.

The *Stena Cambria* arrived for overhaul on 18th October emerging in full Stena Line livery. The name 'Sealink' was dropped at the end of the year.

1996

The *Stena Cambria* returned to Dover to work the 19.00 to Calais on 19th January. and awaiting the arrival of Stena's 'new' *Stena Empereur* (ex *Stena Jutlandica*) on 15th August but in the event she was retained in the Dover Strait to make up her owners' five ship service. She was off service after striking the quayside at Calais on 16th June later sailing to ARNO at Dunkirk for repairs and

During 1996, the **Stena Cambria** *was repainted in the full Stena Line livery and is captured on a blustery day, crossing to Calais. There are not many takers for the Sun Deck! (FotoFlite)*

ST. ANSELM/STENA CAMBRIA

*The **Stena Cambria** is pictured at the Salt Island berth whilst maintaining the Dun Laoghaire route. (Gordon Hislip)*

*With Stena markings painted out, the **Stena Cambria** is seen at the end of her service on the Irish Sea prior to her transfer to the Newhaven-Dieppe route. (Gordon Hislip)*

was back in service on 28th June.

1997

On 11th February the *Stena Parisien* (ex *Champs Elysees*) was handed back to SeaFrance and became their *SeaFrance Manet*. She was replaced on the Newhaven route by the *Stena Cambria* which allowed her sister ship the *Stena Antrim* to depart for refit.

On her initial stern-first departure from the Sussex port, the *Stena Cambria* ran aground on the mud at the harbour entrance for 90 minutes. Later that day she was also delayed in Dieppe with internal ramp problems.

With the *Stena Antrim* back on 23rd February, both ships worked the service until the entry into service of the 81 metre fast craft *Stena Lynx III* on 24th March after which the *Stena Cambria* departed for the Irish Sea.

The ship arrived at Belfast on 27th March and took up service at Stranraer four days later supporting the *Stena Galloway* and *Stena Caledonia*. With the arrival of the HSS *Stena Discovery* on 26th April, the *Stena Cambria* sailed to Holyhead to cover during the period of closure of its own HSS service until 3rd May. It was then to Dover where she took up the Calais service for the final time on 13th May.

Much uncertainly now shrouded the future of the *Stena Cambria* but it seemed fairly certain that she had no long term future in the Stena Line fleet. Her name was linked with the Stena subsidiary Lion

The Saints go marching on

*The **Stena Cambria** enters the River Ouse at Newhaven at the end of a crossing from Dieppe in August 1998. (John Hendy)*

Ferry link between Denmark and Sweden but after the first HSS 1500 catamaran (*Stena Explorer*) had entered service between Holyhead and Dun Laoghaire on 10th April 1996, the writing was most certainly on the wall.

With the creation of the Stena/ P&O European Ferries joint venture in the eastern English Channel on 19th November, her final service was destined to be the Newhaven – Dieppe route which had shown a 62% drop in passengers and a 33% drop in freight in the previous five years.

1998

The *Stena Cambria* refitted between 21st December 1997 and 11th January before replacing her sister during mid-March after which she sailed to Swansea for a final refit. On her return she allowed the *Stena Cambria* to proceed for her own refit during which time she was painted in the new joint-service livery and a return to the blue hull in which she was created. On 24th April she replaced the *Stena Antrim* which sailed for lay-up.

The 81 metre fast craft *Elite* (ex *Stena Lynx III*) had proved inadequate and was beset by so many technical problems that at the close of the season in October P&O Stena Line announced that it would not return to the route. Discussions concerning its future were progressing.

1999

On 15th January, P&O Stena Line announced that the service would close on Sunday 31st January with the *Stena Cambria* laying up at Zeebrugge and her French crew redeployed at Dover.

Following the route's closure, the *Stena Cambria* sailed to Dover's berth 1 to de-store before departing at 13.00 on 2nd February for Zeebrugge. There she was sold to Spanish owners Umafisa and renamed *Isla de Botafoc* before being handed over on 18th February.

Newhaven port's owners, Sea Containers announced that they would take over the seasonal Dieppe route with their monohull *SuperSeaCat Two* as from 23rd April 1999.

ST. CHRISTOPHER/STENA ANTRIM
by John Hendy

London had originally earmarked Dover's second new ferry as the 'St. Augustine' which was a happy choice commemorating the first Archbishop of Canterbury and the man who brought Christianity to England in 597.

However, Dover management immediately expressed concerns regarding the chosen name as to local people, it brought to mind the well-known hospital for the mentally ill on the Downs near Canterbury. In the circumstances, the name *St. Christopher* – the patron saint of travellers – appeared to be a happy compromise, although the name 'St. Dunstan' was also considered.

The *St. Christopher* was due in service with the 01.00 on 28th September but in the event was almost six months late. For the builders, Sir Brian Morton said that were times when building a ship seemed more difficult than sending a man to the moon. He blamed the difficult transition from building 300,000 tankers to smaller-type vessels. Poor weather and problems with one particular sub-contractor did not help Harland & Wolff's case.

For Sealink UK Ltd, Chairman Michael Bosworth stated the obvious, "They are late on delivery. We ordered four ships and the first one is already ten months late. Our competitors bought their ships from Germany and they are not late."

Having previously looked at differences between the four ships of the 'Saint' class, it was stated that in order to save weight, the *St. Christopher*'s solid bulwarks along her Boat Deck were removed by the

Seen just after the new Sun Deck was added astern of the twin funnels, the **St. Christopher** *heads towards Dover. (Sealink UK Ltd)*

The **St. Christopher** at speed and about to enter Dover Harbour on 16th June 1981. (John Hendy)

ST. CHRISTOPHER/STENA ANTRIM

*The **St. Christopher** leaves Fishguard during her spell on the route prior to moving to Dover. (Miles Cowsill)*

shipyard and replaced by railings. Subsequently, the *St. Anselm* was always the better looking of the two ships.

But a stranger change took place shortly after the *St. Christopher* had taken up service at Dover. Apparently unknown to Management and certainly unknown to Senior Master Captain Edwin Venables, sometime during July, the ship's 'A' crew Quartermaster supervised the blue painting of the ship's solid bulwark around her fo'c'sle so that she was quite distinct from the *St. Anselm* whose forward bulwark was always white.

As the monthly ferry correspondent of 'Sea Breezes' magazine between 1976 and 1988, I duly mentioned the curious 'modification' in my 'Ferry Scene' article. When next I travelled with Captain Venables, he told me that he knew nothing about the 'change' until he had read about it. He did, however, approve of the modification!

The launch of the third Townsend Thoresen 'Spirit' class vessel (*Pride of Free Enterprise*) had received much positive publicity when the owners approached the BBC television programme 'Jim'll Fix It.'

This occupied an early Saturday evening peak viewing slot in which viewers were able to write to the presenter Jimmy Saville asking him to 'fix' something for them. A nine-year old schoolgirl asked to launch a ship and the rest is history.

The *St. Christopher* was to become the 'Blue Peter' ship and was adopted by the famous children's television programme. Much art work resulted from the link and the programme followed the ship through all stages of building, via the naming ceremony and launch to dry-dockings and refits. It seemed like a very positive publicity stunt as if parents were to listen to their children, then many families would be looking to cross the Channel via Sealink's latest television 'star.'

1980

In gale-force winds at 12.30 on 18th March, the ship was named by Miss Tina Heath, presenter of the BBC children's television programme 'Blue Peter.' It was not until two days later that the launch took place. There cannot be many instances where the launching of sister ships has been delayed due to gales.

1981

As the ship neared completion at Harland & Wolff, it became increasingly certain that Dover's new ship would be even later than expected.

The Fishguard – Rosslare ferry *Stena Normandica* urgently required a period of relief (it had originally been scheduled for January) and it was planned to introduce the *St. Christopher* onto the St. George's

*The **St. Christopher**, nearing Calais, passes the **St. Anselm** which is heading for Dover in August 1981. The blue-painted forward bulwark is very obvious. (John Hendy)*

Channel route to allow maintenance to take place to the chartered Stena ship.

The *St. Christopher* duly left Harland & Wolff on 14th March and sailed directly for Rosslare (County Wexford) for ramp tests. At this time, the Holyhead – Dun Laoghaire ferry *St. Coumba* was also experiencing engine troubles and promptly broke down yet again. In a hasty piece of reorganisation, the *St. Christopher* was sailed back up the Irish coast to Dun Laoghaire (County Dublin) and thence to Holyhead where she arrived at midnight on 15th March. After moving to the repair berth at 07.00 the following morning, the ship's maiden voyage was duly carried out with the afternoon sailing from Holyhead on 17th March.

Two days later she sailed to Fishguard and took the 14.45 to Rosslare, remaining there until relieved by the errant *Stena Normandica* on 12th April.

The *St. Christopher* left for Dover two hours later arriving at her home port at 14.00 on the following day. She completed her third maiden voyage in less than a month when she took the 08.15 from Dover to Calais on 15th April allowing the relieving SNCF car ferry *Chantilly* to stand-down.

Continuing the work of her sister ship, during the first week of November, and with two RMT ferries off service, the *St. Christopher*

ST. CHRISTOPHER/STENA ANTRIM

was switched to run overnight Dover – Ostend sailings departing Dover at 22.30 and returning from the Belgian port at 07.00. SNCF's *Chantilly* was brought in to run the missed overnight sailings to Calais.

At the end of the year the ship was noted as sailing without the white-painted steel BR logo on her starboard funnel.

1982

As with the *St. Anselm*, the *St. Christopher* also had her Bridge Deck aft of the twin funnels opened up to passenger use and certificates were raised from 1,000 to 1,200.

The head-on collision between SNCF's *Cote d'Azur* and *Chantilly* off Calais in the early hours of 5th August caused severe problems to the Sealink schedules.

Shortly afterwards, the *St. Christopher* failed with serious crankshaft problems and the *Horsa* was switched from her Folkestone – Boulogne schedules in order to keep the Dover – Calais service operational while the former Dieppe-based SNCF ferry *Villandry* was moved to cover the Folkestone - Boulogne link. After a period at the Admiralty Pier's berth 5, on 25th August the *St. Christopher* sailed for the calmer waters of Ostend's deep-water berth with an extra crew who bought back the spare Belgian ferry *Roi Baudouin* to work the Dover – Boulogne service. The *St. Christopher* was back at Dover on 14th October. How fortunate that spare ships were available!

A quick visit to Tilbury was necessary for belting repairs immediately after Christmas and on her return to service, the *St. Anselm* sailed for modifications at Belfast.

1983

With the *St. Anselm* back at Belfast receiving an extension to her

*In dry dock at Chatham in January 1985, the **St. Christopher** shows her weather proof bow visor, water tight doors and her bow rudder. (John Hendy)*

The Saints go marching on

*The **St. Christopher** arriving at Calais on 2nd November 1981. Notice the absence of the steel BR double-arrow logo from the starboard funnel which had recently fallen off! (John Hendy)*

passenger accommodation during the first quarter of the year, Sealink transferred the *St. David* from the Irish Sea to cover the *St. Christopher*'s refit. After a brief call at Falmouth, under the command of Captain George Sutcliffe, the fourth of the 'Saints' took up the 13.00 to Calais on 31st March. With the *St. Christopher* returning to Dover on 9th June and taking up the 17.30 to Calais, the *St. David* sailed back to the Irish Sea.

Passenger certificates were raised to 1,400 but were subsequently lowered to 1,350. Gross tonnage was raised to 7,399.

1984

Industrial action at Calais on 25th – 26th May saw both Dover 'Saints' sailing to Boulogne although a break-down to the *St. Christopher* saw the *Chantilly* deputising on the second day.

The closure of the Folkestone – Calais service and the introduction of a four ship Dover – Calais link to include the train-connected services provided by the Folkestone route caused chaos when it was introduced on 3rd June.

Certain sailings were switched to the Admiralty Pier (Western Docks) linkspan to connect with the trains using the Marine station and the *St. Christopher* was scheduled to work once of them. The ship immediately proved herself to be totally inept at handling large numbers of foot passengers and their luggage and turn round times were delayed. There was simply no where within the ship's accommodation to store all the baggage and the narrowness of the Admiralty pier berth prohibited the ship from serving as a drive-

69

ST. CHRISTOPHER/STENA ANTRIM

In readiness for privatisation in 1984, Sealink UK ships had their railway 'double arrow' symbols removed from their funnels. (John Hendy)

through vessel as her stern failed to fit. All lorries therefore to reverse on board causing further delays. So much for progress!

Sea Containers purchased Sealink UK Ltd during July for £66 million: 37 ships, 10 harbours and 24 routes.

1985

Arriving on 23rd January, the *St. Christopher* dry-docked in the former naval dockyard at Thames Ship Repairers, Chatham.

On 20th June, a short strike at Calais saw the *St. Christopher* crossing from Dover to Boulogne.

1986

The *St. Christopher* followed the *St. Anselm* to Meyer's yard at Papenburg, West Germany in order to receive £1.5 million of improvements to her accommodation. The *Vortigern* was brought in on 6th April to take her roster.

The *Vortigern* again deputised for the *St. Christopher* when the latter ship went off service with crankshaft problems in October.

The *St. Christopher* was again off service with crankshaft problems in late October and work was carried out in the Camber at Dover. The *Vortigern* was called to deputise until 17th November after which she retired to the Wellington Dock.

1987

On 16th October, during the morning of the Great Storm when hurricane-force winds were lashing the south of England and the

The Saints go marching on

*Following the purchase by Stena Line in 1990, the Sealink fleet was styled 'Sealink Stena Line' The **Stena Antrim** is thus adorned after her renaming in 1991. (FotoFlite)*

Hengist was aground in the Warren, the *St. Christopher* left Calais for Dover at 03.00 but was unable to enter the port. She therefore headed northwards to an area known as the Downs, which is a sheltered anchorage between Deal and the Goodwin Sands, in order to ride out the storm. On turning about, she was hit by seas of such force that the steel door on her upper vehicle or B Deck was split open and some of her cargo overturned. After a nine hour crossing from Calais, the ship eventually reached Dover where the clear-up operations began.

With Folkestone closed due to the tremendous damage to the station, pier and ro-ro installations, the *Horsa* was transferred to the Dover – Calais link vice the *St. Christopher*.

ST. CHRISTOPHER/STENA ANTRIM

1989

As early as 1989, there was a degree of uncertainty regarding the ship's future with Sealink examining options to switch her to the Newhaven – Dieppe link and run her in tandem with the *Versailles* (later *SeaFrance Monet*). The plan was that she should replace the *Chartres* which should return to the Dover Strait to operate the seasonal Dover Western Docks – Calais train-connected services. The French were not impressed and wished for the *Cote d'Azur* to be switched to Dieppe leaving the *St. Christopher* on the Calais link.

1990

The converted deep-sea ro-ro vessels *Fantasia* and SNAT"s *Fiesta* appeared on the Dover – Calais service in March and May.

Stena Line acquired Sealink British Ferries for £259 million during April. The company was renamed Sealink Stena Line and a re-evaluation of routes and ships was immediately ordered.

1991

The *St. Christopher* arrived back at Dover from overhaul named *Stena Antrim* in readiness for her transfer to the North Channel route linking Stranraer and Larne. At the conclusion of her afternoon sailing from Calais on 4th April, the ship de-stored before heading for the Irish Sea. She was replaced at Dover by the *Stena Cambria*.

The *Stena Antrim* entered service on her new route with the 09.30 from Stranraer to Larne on 7th April replacing the *Darnia* on the quietest and least demanding of the port's three rosters.. Her new operational partners were the *Stena Galloway* (ex *Galloway Princess*) and the *Stena Caledonia* (ex *St. David*).

In late 1993, the company name was again restyled. The **Stena Antrim** *arrives at Holyhead in Stena Sealink livery in 18th January 1995. (Gordon Hislip)*

1992

During annual refit the *Stena Antrim* was re-registered at Stranraer.

1993

During November, the company was restyled Stena Sealink Line.

1995

The *Stena Antrim* covered refits at both Holyhead (relieving the *Stena Hibernia* on 4th January and then the *Stena Cambria*) and Fishguard. Following this stint, she sailed to Birkenhead for her own overhaul returning to Stranraer on 27th February.

On 6th April the ship sailed for Newhaven (arrived the next day) via Belfast for berthing trials to cover the 15-day refit refit of the *Stena Parisien*.

On 11th November she completed the final crossing between Stranraer and Larne before the Ulster terminal was switched to Belfast on the following day.'

At the end of the year the name 'Sealink' was dropped and the company became known as Stena Line.

1996

Following the introduction of the HSS *Stena Voyager* on the Stranraer – Belfast service on 21st July, the 14-year old *Stena Antrim* was spare and laid-up at Belfast. However, operational problems were to beset the new craft and with her high wash characteristics causing environmental problems to the shores of Loch Ryan and Belfast Lough, timings had to be amended as a result of which she lost a daily sailing. The *Stena Antrim* was subsequently brought out of retirement to provide extra support on the route.

Much uncertainly continued to shroud the future of the *Stena Antrim* but it seemed fairly certain that she had no long term future in the Stena Line fleet. With the creation of the Stena/ P&O European Ferries joint venture in the English Channel, her final service was on the Newhaven – Dieppe route on which she appeared during November.

1997

On 11th February the *Stena Parisien* (ex *Champs Elysees*) was handed back to SeaFrance and became their *SeaFrance Manet* at Calais. She was replaced on the Newhaven route by the *Stena Cambria* which allowed the *Stena Antrim* to sail for refit returning on 23rd February at

The **Stena Antrim** makes an unusual sight at Newhaven whilst working the route in 1997. The 'Antrim' is pictured leaving for Dieppe. (John Bryant)

17.00. Both sisters worked the route until the arrival of the fast craft *Stena Lynx III* (renamed *Elete*) on 24th March after which the *Stena Cambria* returned to the Irish Sea to cover refits.

1998

During mid-March the *Stena Cambria* again replaced her sister which went off for a refit at Swansea. On her return she allowed the 'Cambria' to refit but on her arrival back at Newhaven on 24th April, the *Stena Antrim* was withdrawn and sailed to Zeebrugge to lay-up pending sale.

On 11th June she was sold to Limadet of Morocco and was renamed *Ibn Batouta* sailing two days later for conversion at Cadiz.

ST. DAVID/STENA CALEDONIA
by Miles Cowsill

The *St. David* was the fourth in the series of vessels built for Sealink UK Ltd and was originally ordered to replace the *Stena Normandica* on the Fishguard-Rosslare route. In the event she was to start her career at Holyhead. During her construction a stern bridge was provided to enable her to berth more easily at Holyhead and an additional public room was provided for her role on the Holyhead-Dun Laoghaire service. As with the three earlier vessels in the class, the *St. David* was delayed entering service by some 10 months.

1981

The *St. David* entered service under the command of Captain Idwal Pritchard on 10th August. Her passenger accommodation differed from the *St. Anselm* and *St. Christopher*, in that she was designed for the longer Irish Sea crossings. Her accommodation allowed for a restaurant forward, a cinema and the lounge bar on the Upper Deck. The vessel was also to incorporate a supermarket instead of the old counter system which was a feature of the Dover sisters. The internal vehicle ramps used on the *St. David* gave access to both decks in the absence of a double-decked linkspan at either Holyhead or Dun Laoghaire at the time.

On the arrival of the *St. David*, the chartered *Prinsessan Desiree*, which had been covering for her late arrival into service, stood down. During September it was announced that the *St. David* would operate

*The **St. David** arrives on her inaugural voyage at the port of Holyhead. (Dick Richards)*

in place of the *St. Columba* during the winter as she was a more economic vessel to operate off-season with better freight capacity. Arguably a ro-pax before her time?

1982

The *St. David* was prevented from entering the port of Dun Laoghaire, during a period of unrest between Sealink and the their rivals B+I, when the B+I vessel *Munster* blocked the entrance to the harbour - see page 83. During the *St. David*'s overhaul at Avonmouth, internal alterations were made to her accommodation and meanwhile the *St. Columba* covered for her absence. Once again she entered full operations at Holyhead during the summer period until early

Crowds on the quayside see of the last of the quartet being launched at Harland & Wolff. (Ferry Publications Library)

ST. DAVID/STENA CALEDONIA

*The **St. David** arrives at Larne in January 1984. Originally the vessel had been intended to commence commercial service between Fishguard and Rosslare. (Ken Kane)*

October.

Passenger carryings on the Holyhead-Dun Laoghaire route increased by some 11.4% during 1982 with the two-ship operation at the port.

In October, the *St. Columba* was sent for overhaul and conversion to a one-class vessel, when her place was taken by the *Ailsa Princess*.

1983

The *St. David* was sent to Stranraer to cover for the refits on the North Channel. She then sailed to cover the overhaul of the *Stena Normandica* on the Fishguard-Rosslare service in February. Following her stint on the St. George's Channel, she then sailed south to Dover to cover for the major overhauls of the *St. Anselm* and *St. Christopher*, entering service between Dover and Calais on the 13.00 sailing on 31st March, just in time for the Easter rush.

The *St. David* remained on the English Channel until 7th June when following her stint on the English Channel she was sent for a short overhaul before entering service again at Holyhead route with the *St. Columba*.

1984

The *St. David* sailed north again to cover for the refits at Stranraer. In a surprise move, she was sent to Harwich to cover for the absence of the *St. Nicholas* from 8th March for three weeks. Whilst she was operating on the North Sea operations for Sealink, she was mainly employed to run in tandem with the *Koningin Juliana* as a freight vessel carrying freight drivers at night and only a few passengers on the daylight sailings from Harwich to the Hook of Holland.

1985

In line with other ships in the fleet, the *St. David* appeared in the new livery of Sealink British Ferries following Sea Containers purchase of the Sealink UK operations. At the same time it was announced that the *St. David* would be transferred to Dover as from 21st March to operate on the joint service with RTM to Ostend. She was earmarked to operate in tandem with the Belgian vessels *Stena Nautica* and *Reine Astrid*. The *St. David*'s crossing time between Dover and Ostend was scheduled to 4 hours 15 minutes. The *St. David* was also employed from 1st July to 28th September on the Dover-Boulogne service on Saturdays in place of the SNCF ferry *Champs Elysees* which maintained the link during weekdays and Sundays.

With Captain George Sutcliffe in command, the **St. David** *sweeps into Calais for the first time on 31st March 1983. (John Hendy)*

ST. DAVID/STENA CALEDONIA

*The **St. David** leaving Dover for Calais on 3rd April 1983 vice the **St. Christopher** which was back at Belfast having her after accommodation extended. (the late Dr. P. Ransome-Wallis)*

Prior to her move to Dover, she stood in again for the *Stena Normandica* at Fishguard.

As a result of Sealink's new owners placing the *St. David* on the Ostend link and pressure by Sealink to have a greater stake in freight traffic on the Belgian route, the joint partnership between Sealink and RTM came to end. Meanwhile, the Belgians entered into a new trading agreement with Townsend Thoresen, which in turn bared Sealink from operating to Ostend.

1986

In April, the *St. David* was once again back on the Irish Sea covering for the *St. Columba*, whilst she went to Germany for a major refit. On her return the *St. David* sailed north to join the *Galloway Princess* and the *Darnia* on the Larne – Stranraer service.

The Saints go marching on

*In 1985 the **St. David** operated from Dover to Ostend. She is seen at lay-by on Dover's Admiralty Pier prior to loading at the Eastern Docks.. (Miles Cowsill)*

*The **St David** receiving her annual overhaul at Swansea Docks in April 1986. (Miles Cowsill)*

1987

The *St. David* returned to the Holyhead-Dun Laoghaire route from 27th February to 12th March, to cover for the *St. Columba*. For the next two years she remained an integral part of the Stranraer-Larne service, which continued to see growth of freight and passenger traffic.

1989

The *St. David* remained at Stranraer and was replaced on overhaul by the train ferry *Saint Eloi*, which proved an unpopular choice of stand-in vessel.

1990

In April the hostile take-over battle for Sea Containers was finally resolved with Sealink British Ferries' operations being acquired by Stena Line. The Swedish company began a thorough re-evaluation of all ships and routes. The most outward sign of change was the re-branding of the company as Sealink Stena Line. The *St. David* was renamed *Stena Caledonia* as part of the changes by the Swedish company. She was also re-registered to the port of Stranraer. Another unsuitable ship was sent to cover for the absence of the 'Caledonia' in 1990: the *Earl Granville*. A second ship, the veteran *Cambridge Ferry*, was also deployed to give freight support to the *Earl Granville*.

79

ST. DAVID/STENA CALEDONIA

*The **Stena Caledonia** makes a fine view here at Belfast on her afternoon lay-over at the port. (Gordon Hislip)*

*The **Stena Caledonia** dressed overall whilst being chartered by the Tour de France organisation in 1997. (Gordon Hislip)*

This year saw the *St. Christopher* (now renamed *Stena Antrim*) being transferred from Dover to the Stranraer-Larne route to offer extra capacity and replacing the *Darnia* in the local fleet.

1995

The three 'Saint' class ships maintained operations between Stranraer-Larne together for the next five years in a perfect partnership, being three ships of similar design which could, if required, be switched around on rosters without disruption to customers or stand in if one vessel had to be withdrawn from service for repairs. At the start of 1994 it was becoming clear that Stena Line planned to move their Irish port from Larne to Belfast, pending the arrival of the HSS craft for the route. On 12th November the *Stena Antrim* made the last crossing from Larne. As a result of the move the schedules became more intensive with the longer sea passages involved.

1996

The *Stena Voyager* (the second HSS) commenced commercial service on 21st July. The new roster allowed the *Stena Caledonia* to operate a rotating roster with the *Stena Galloway*. Passengers and their cars were encouraged to use the new HSS operation which in turn saw fewer passengers using the conventional ships. By the autumn both vessels were operating purely as freight ships.

Due to major mechanical problems in October the *Stena Caledonia* had to be withdrawn from operations. Her place was taken by the now redundant *Stena Adventurer* (ex *St. Columba*, *Stena Hibernia*) from Holyhead, operating her last sailings for the company prior to her sale to Agapitos Express Ferries.

1997

On 30th March, the *Stena Voyager* (HSS) was withdrawn from the Belfast service for a month and once again the conventional ships were left to maintain the route with the *Stena Cambria*.

1998

The *Koningin Beatrix* was due to refit on 6th January and was replaced by the *Stena Caledonia* on the Fishguard-Rosslare route. Her time on the Southern Corridor was short-lived as she had to return to the Stranraer-Belfast link after the *Stena Voyager* was transferred to the Harwich-Hook of Holland route, following major mechanical

*This view shows the **Stena Caledonia** following her SOLAS modifications to her stern leaving Stranraer for Belfast. (Miles Cowsill)*

problems with the third HSS, *Stena Discovery*. The 'Cambria' was consequently transferred from Dover in place of the 'Caledonia' at Fishguard.

In July the *Stena Caledonia*, the *Koningin Beatrix* (Fishguard-Rosslare) and the *Stena Challenger* (Holyhead-Dublin), were chartered to sail from Ireland to France to convey the support teams and their crews of the 'Tour de France'. The 'Caledonia' sailed from Rosslare to Roscoff, while the other two Stena vessels sailed from Cork. All three ships conveyed over 2,000 tour personnel, TV crews and media, as well as hundreds of cars, vans, lorries and a hospitality unit.

ST. DAVID/STENA CALEDONIA

*The **Stena Caledonia** has on a couple of occasions maintained the Fishguard-Rosslare route. She is seen here at the port of Rosslare whilst covering for the **Stena Europe** in 2005. (Gordon Hislip)*

1999

The *Stena Caledonia* was sent for refit at Cammell Laird in February for a month during which the sponsons were fitted to her stern to bring her up to SOLAS requirements. In addition during this refit, her bow rudder is removed and a new bulbous bow is constructed.

During April, Stena Line announced that they planned to move back to Larne with their conventional vessels on the Stranraer service, the *Stena Caledonia* and *Stena Galloway*, however nothing ever became of these plans despite the 'Caledonia' undertaking berthing trials on 5th October 1999.

2005

After almost seven years on the Stranraer-Belfast route, the *Stena Caledonia* was sent once again to Fishguard to cover the Rosslare service, ironically the service for which she was initially intended. The 'Caledonia' covered for the *Stena Europe* between 19th May and 12th July. Meanwhile, the *Stena Seafarer* covered for the absence of the 'Caledonia' on the Stranraer-Belfast route.

ST. DAVID BLOCKADE
by Justin Merrigan

The announcement of B+I Line's intention to open a new route between Dublin and Holyhead in March 1982 provoked an angry response from the Welsh side of the Irish Sea. Sealink port workers at Holyhead, fearful for their livelihoods, immediately refused to handle the B+I ship, threatening to "line the quays" if she appeared off the port. Appear she did on 28th February and having been met by a blockade of small boats across the mouth of the inner harbour, she was forced to return to Dublin having failed in her attempts to carry out berthing trials.

On 2nd March the inaugural commercial sailing was cancelled as attempts to break the deadlock commenced but by 8th March progress had still not been made and with B+I determined to open their new route the *Connacht* once again sailed for Holyhead. On arrival off the port she was again faced with the full fury of port workers and after an hour and a half waiting outside Capt Frank

*With port engine going astern, the **St David** squares up to B+I Line's **Munster** on a first attempt to break the blockade on 8th March 1982. (Justin Merrigan Collection)*

Devaney had no alternative but to return to Dublin.

As a schoolboy, Dun Laoghaire Harbour was my playground and as Ireland emerged from a long dark winter the stretching spring evenings enticed me to the port to watch the early evening arrival of *St. David* from Holyhead in daylight. While making my way towards the Carlisle Pier I stopped at the head of the East Pier to survey the scene. It was there I overheard a group of men discussing plans to block the harbour entrance with a number of "inflatables and perhaps the *Tipperary* to help us", the latter

ST. DAVID BLOCKADE

being B+I's Dublin – Fleetwood ro-ro vessel.

Immediately, I informed the Harbour Police who, I am sure, did not believe what I had to say. However, if they did doubt me then their misgivings were to be shortlived. The repeated failure of their ships to berth at Holyhead led B+I crews to take retaliatory action. While the *Connacht* was returning to Dublin a crew boarded the laid-up *Munster* and sailed her across Dublin Bay to Dun Laoghaire where she dropped anchor in the mouth of the harbour. The intentions of her crew were simply to prevent access to any Sealink vessel.

With a one hour and thirty minute head start over the returning *Connacht*, Sealink's *St. David* approached Dublin Bay at 18.00 to find her way into the harbour well and truly blocked.

I can recall this most incredible sight. Seeing the blue and white-hulled *Munster* sailing across Dublin Bay towards Dun Laoghaire was unusual in itself, but to then watch as she slowed and manoeuvred across the mouth of the harbour seemed quite surreal.

On the bridge of the approaching *St. David* there was a similar feeling as Capt. Idwal Pritchard and his officers looked at ways of berthing the ship at Dun Laoghaire. Calling the *Munster* by VHF radio to ask of their intentions, Capt. Pritchard was initially met with silence but the Irish ship eventually indicated they would not be moving. Asking if the *Munster* was anchored, the *St. David* was given a blunt, "Yes!"

Then followed the first of several attempts to break the blockade. The *St. David* went for a gap between the *Munster's* bow and the East Pier lighthouse, prompting a warning from the *Munster's* Master that small boats were placed between his ship and the wall. The *St. David* moved astern and coming to rest about a ship's length from the anchored vessel. She then made another run for a gap between the *Munster's* stern and the West Pier but using her engines, the B+I ship moved to block the ship again. Still the *St. David* continued her approach, finally coming to a halt seemingly within a few feet of the *Munster*. The Irish ship was completely dwarfed but nonetheless unperturbed by the 'David'. After a few breath-taking moments the *St. David* again moved astern.

From ashore there was no doubt; the *Munster* had placed both herself and the *St. David* in a highly dangerous situation. The *St. David* being a highly manoeuvrable vessel, Capt. Pritchard had full command of his ship and was able to do exactly what he wanted with her.

Clearly audible from the decks of the *St. David* were the chants of 38 school children crying "Sealink, Sealink!" The children, aged between 11 and 12, were on a school rugby excursion and were catered for by the ship's Chief Steward and his crew.

This game of cat and mouse continued for well over an hour but each time the *Munster* thwarted the British ship's attempts. Finally, shortly before midnight the *St. David* returned to Holyhead for stores and a reappraisal of the situation.

Meanwhile, Sealink's Managing Director Len Merryweather stressed to staff that his company was legally obliged to permit any operator to use its port facilities. He insisted that Sealink had not approached B+I with an offer to enter Holyhead, a fact equally confirmed by the Irish company. "If Sealink adopt restrictive practices to B+I they must expect similar restrictive practices to be imposed upon Sealink in Irish Ports." "The interests of the company and the staff lies in correctly handling the B+I service from the outset," he said.

The following morning, with Captain Pritchard once again on the

The Saints go marching on

with starboard engine problems on 13th September and their *Prins Albert* also out of service since 1st September, the *St. Anselm* was diverted from her Calais services to operate overnight from Dover to Ostend.

The arrival of the *Cote d'Azur* in service on 7th October allowed the *St. Anselm* to depart for a three-day refit at Dunkirk.

1982

During the spring, SNCF Armement Naval ordered a sister ship for the *Cote d'Azur* with the intention of running her from Dover to Boulogne. The service had long ceased to be an important part of Sealink's long-term plans and was now very much a subsidiary route on which the older and smaller ferries operated.

*The **St. Anselm** and her SNCF partner **Cote d'Azur** (now the **SeaFrance Renior**) rest between trips in the inner port as the dredger keeps the harbour clear. (Calais Chamber of Commerce)*

With a passenger certificate for as many as 1,800 the new vessel would present a great imbalance alongside the British Rail twins with their 1,000 passenger certificates. Plans were therefore put in hand to increase accommodation by 200.

This was achieved by opening up the Bridge Deck aft of the twin funnels, providing fixed-seating and clear, plastic sheeting across the new railings. The extra accommodation proved very popular providing excellent viewing and protection from the wind. Further plans were announced to increase the certificates to 1,400 by extending the accommodation aft and providing a self-service duty-free area.

The ship was off service with mechanical problems on 13th August.

The *St. Anselm* was again off service with engine troubles and was sent to Dunkirk from 1st November. The problems involved a crankshaft and had been anticipated following serious problems with the *St. Christopher* earlier in the season. SNCF's *Chantilly* deputised on the Dover – Calais route while Sealink chartered the spare Belgian ferry *Roi Baudouin* to keep the Folkestone – Boulogne service operational.

After completing service three days after Christmas, the *St. Anselm* was sent back to Harland & Wolff at Belfast on 31st December for her accommodation extension to be fitted. Initial plans for the Boat Deck tea bar to be converted into a waiter-service restaurant came to nothing. In any case, as the area was not fire proofed, only cold, but more substantial, meals could be served. Visually, the main difference was the extension of the accommodation right to the stern and the creation of a self-service duty-free area. Gross tonnage was increased by 402: from 7,003 to 7,405.

The **St. Christopher** *arrives off the entrance to the Eastern Docks at Dover inward-bound from Calais. Astern of her can be seen the* **Vortigern** *which was maintaining the Dunkirk train ferry service. (Miles Cowsill)*

*The **St. Anselm** arrives at Dover Western Docks in 1984 on the train-connected service from Calais prior to being repainted in Sealink British Ferries' livery. (Miles Cowsill).*

The **St. Christopher** *looking her best as she storms up between the jetties at Calais. (John Hendy)*

The **St. David** emerges from the spring mist at Larne inward-bound from Stranraer. (Miles Cowsill)

Photography at the end of the west pier at Calais can be hazardous with fishermen and their rods frequently in evidence. The **Stena Cambria** *at speed makes an impressive view as she butts into the seas in 1992. (John Hendy)*

The **Stena Cambria** arrives at Holyhead inward-bound from Dun Laoghaire. The vessel was ultimately withdrawn from Irish Sea services on the entry into service of the HSS. *(Miles Cowsill)*

*The **Stena Cambria** arrives at Holyhead in Stena Sealink Line livery whilst operating on the Central Corridor prior to the arrival of the HSS. (Miles Cowsill)*

The *Stena Antrim* glides into Larne from Stranraer in the evening sunlight. (Miles Cowsill)

With a peaceful-looking Loch Ryan and the open sea astern, the **Stena Caledonia** *on her berth at Stranraer prior to her afternoon crossing to Belfast in September 2000. (John Hendy)*

Taken from Dover Harbour Board's hydrographic survey launch, the **Stena Cambria** *leaving Dover for Calais in October 1997 during one of her final spells on the route for which she was built. (John Hendy)*

The **Stena Galloway** *(ex **Galloway Princess**) heads out of Loch Ryan for Belfast. (Miles Cowsill)*

The **Stena Caledonia** *(ex **St. David**) arrives at Larne during her last season operating to the Antrim port prior to Stena Line moving its operations to Belfast. (Miles Cowsill)*

The **Stena Antrim** at Newhaven in 1997 whilst covering for the absence of her sister the **Stena Cambria**. (John Bryant)

*Almost of end for the **Stena Cambria** but looking very smart in her joint-service livery, the French-crewed ship has just arrived at Newhaven from Dieppe in August 1998. The funnel extensions were a very late addition. (John Hendy)*

*The **Stena Caledonia** passes Cairnryan outward-bound to Belfast prior to her conversion and upgrading to SOLAS specifications. (Miles Cowsill)*

The Saints go marching on

*Captured passing Cairnryan against the afternoon sun, the **Stena Caledonia** heads out of Loch Ryan bound for Belfast. (John Hendy)*

bridge, the *St. David* reappeared off Dun Laoghaire once again finding the *Munster* firmly blockading the harbour entrance. However, by now the Sealink ferry had a sick passenger on board and following a doctor's call for urgent medical treatment the *Munster* moved aside on humanitarian grounds. Sailing through the harbour entrance at a rate of knots the *St. David* quickly proceeded to her Carlisle Pier berth. An awaiting ambulance reversed up the linkspan and onto the vehicle deck, the casualty being taken to hospital away from the full glare of media attention. After a very quick turnaround the *St. David* sailed again for Holyhead and with all sailings suspended until further notice the B+I ship returned to her berth in Dublin.

On 7th April B+I's *Leinster* finally entered Holyhead unopposed. Reinstated members of the National Union of Railwaymen who had previously been dismissed for refusing to work B+I ships handled her at the station berth. With the Welsh Dragon and the Red Ensign flying from her mast the *Leinster* occupied the berth vacated 30 minutes earlier by the *St Columba*. Holyhead's link with Ireland was reopened after one long month without sailings.

It is doubtful if such a spectacle will ever be seen again.

85

RECALLING THE SEALINK 'SAINTS'
by Captain Murray Paterson

My first memory of a Saint class vessel (as they were later to be called) was in April 1980 when from my home in Port Glasgow I watched the brand new *Galloway Princess* making her way up the River Clyde to Glasgow on a publicity visit shortly before she was due to begin operating on the Stranraer - Larne service. At this time I was just a few days away from taking up an appointment as Second Officer on the same route and it never crossed my mind that twelve years on this vessel would be my first command in the Company or that I would serve on all three of her sisters; two of them as Master.

The 'Galloway' started on the Larne service a week after I did and although it was some time before I was able to set foot aboard, she certainly dwarfed the two traditional mail boats on which I was then serving and effortlessly swallowed up amazing amounts of cargo on her two vehicle decks. In time I did find myself rostered to the "Big G" and in the pecking order then prevailing, there was certainly a feeling of having made it to the flagship.

At this time our only acquaintance with the other ships of the class were brief glimpses as they came and went from Belfast Lough during their trials and it was to be late 1982 before circumstances brought one of them scurrying north to take the place of the *Antrim Princess* which was off service after a fire. The ship in question was the *St. David* and she was immediately popular with all who served on her. The *St. David* returned the following year as our drydock relief ship.

Nominally a sister of the 'Galloway', the *St. David* was very different in many ways. The cavernous and easy to load car decks were broadly similar but her passenger accommodation had an entirely different layout and reflected the need of other routes to satisfy duty-free requirements which the Stranraer - Larne route did not have. Externally, the *St. David*'s lounges came right out to the hull just forward and aft of the funnels but perhaps the most noticeable difference was the addition of an after bridge and the fact that the main bridge was a deck higher up. The latter feature was greatly appreciated by watch keepers and Masters alike as it placed them above lifeboat level and gave a much improved view. Less obvious to the casual observer was the 'Galloway's' bulbous bow while the *St. David*'s stem incorporated a bow rudder which was not much used in the early years up north. However, the bow rudders fitted to the three later 'Saints' proved a popular asset when they started operating to Belfast in 1995 and were routinely obliged to turn and reverse up to the berth. In defence of the 'Galloway', many felt that her bulbous bow made her more comfortable in a seaway, but it could be a nuisance when berthing and resulted in the ship always having to operate stern in when transferred to the Holyhead - Dun Laoghaire route in 1992. Perhaps more importantly the 'Galloway' had much less power in her engines and bow thrusts with the result lots of us had occasion to envy the other vessels on many a windy winter's night.

The annual refit was one of the highlights in our calendar and this could see us visit such diverse places as Glasgow, Birkenhead, Swansea, Avonmouth, Belfast or even Bremerhaven in Germany. We were in the latter location on the *St. David* having a rather fraught time in 1989 when the first Comic Relief Day took place, and to the astonishment of the Germans the ship was provided with a red nose and a modest sum raised for the good cause. There was a wicked rumour that some personnel had worked hard to acquire red noses in their off-duty time,

The Saints go marching on

but I'm sure that there could be no truth in such a cruel slur!

On a less happy note, on the return from Germany the *St. David* suffered an engine seizure in the southern Irish Sea and had to limp into Liverpool for repair. The problem was soon rectified but eerily as we were about to let go and head home the other engine failed and this took longer to fix.

With so many crew living locally, Glasgow was a popular place for docking though possibly not always the most secure and it seems the *Galloway Princess* inadvertently donated several TV sets to local homes. On another occasion the somewhat elderly night watchman saw, but was unable to stop, some local youths removing large brass bolts from the drydock floor. Before the *St. David*'s propellor blades could be refitted a car had to be dispatched to Stranraer for replacements. While the Master's toilet was being refurbished during one of the 'Galloway's' refits, the removal of deck tiles and cement screed revealed some serious corrosion on the deck below. As this was being inspected the Senior Chief Engineer happened upon the scene and in terms of resigned disappointment directed at Masters in general and no-one in particular, muttered, "Is it any wonder that they miss the piers when they cannot even hit the toilet!"

As privatisation appeared over the horizon in 1984 the ships were given new liveries to symbolise the break from British Rail and the first stage of this was the removal of BR's logo from the funnels. The following year it was goodbye to red funnels and monastral blue hulls and hello to all white-topped with a dark (roundal) blue funnel sporting the new "galloping maggot" logo. For all the longer serving "railway children" these changes were a bit of a wrench, but for the Chief Officers, bosuns and deck crews charged with maintaining the white in good condition life was suddenly more challenging.

*The **Galloway Princess** pictured early in her career on the Stranraer-Larne route. (Captain Murray Paterson)*

As the two Dover 'Saints' were displaced by larger vessels they too found themselves on Irish Sea routes by which time all had been renamed to reflect the style of our second new owners, Stena Line. Only the *Stena Galloway* kept some semblance of her original name though pleasingly the *St. David* became the *Stena Caledonia*, a name harking back to the *Caledonian Princess* which had revitalised the route in the 60's.

Gradually the colour schemes and logos evolved until the full Stena Line livery was achieved, though just before that the decision had been taken to forsake Larne in favour of Belfast and the service was now in the hands of three Saints; the former *St. Christopher* now renamed *Stena Antrim* having joined the 'Galloway' and 'Caledonia'. The *Stena Antrim*

RECALLING THE 'SAINTS'

as the *St. Christopher* had famously been the ship launched by a presenter of the BBC children's TV programme "Blue Peter", - and had a Blue Peter badge (plaque) to prove it - so from time to time while conducting a bridge visit it was appropriate to point to the passing 'Galloway' and say, "and here's one we made earlier".

My first spell of command came in January 1992 when I was to do a week as night Master on the *Stena Galloway*. The possibility of me doing this week had been long flagged up, but as the time drew closer it did tend to concentrate the mind and I was ever aware that January is not always blessed with good weather. In the event it was a placid and incident free seven days at the end of which I gleefully went home elated and relieved - though probably not quite as relieved as Captain Iain McLean the day Master and my unofficial minder.

The *Stena Cambria* (ex *St. Anselm*), the fourth ship of the class also began to feature as a relief ship and was the only one of the quartet to appear in Larne sporting the full Stena colours before the move to Belfast was made on 11th November 1995.

We were sorry to leave Larne. It was a pleasant little town and most of us had cut our ship-handling teeth going in and out of its harbour where strong tides ebbed and flowed through the narrow entrance.

For Belfast, the Masters and Mates had to obtain pilotage exemptions certificates and to this end the ships would spend off service times at the weekends going up and down the channel in order to get the required number of trips in before presenting ourselves for the examination.

The move to Belfast was necessitated by the Company's decision to locate the berth for the new HSS craft there, and in the eight months or so before its introduction the 'Antrim', 'Caledonia' and 'Galloway' (plus the 'Cambria' deputising as relief) ran intensively on a tight and

*The **Stena Cambria** at Belfast in March 1997 whilst serving on the Stranraer route. (Captain Murray Paterson)*

demanding schedule to establish the new route. It says much for the hard work and professionalism of ship and shore staff alike that this was managed in the way it was, but the 'Saints' were up for it even if the slower 'Galloway' did struggle on occasions.

With the HSS *Stena Voyager* in place, the *Stena Antrim* eventually left the route.

During the early part of 2000, the *Stena Caledonia* went to Cammell Laird's at Birkenhead for annual overhaul and major structural changes designed to meet new stability criteria laid down in the Stockholm Agreement. This saw the ship emerge shorn of its bow rudder - a sad loss - but with the addition of a large bulbous bow and a new "bustle" around the stern area. Neither have done much for her appearance but

The Saints go marching on

*This interesting view shows the **Stena Antrim** and the **Stena Caledonia** at Belfast in August 1996. Shortly after this picture was taken the **Stena Antrim** was sold for further service in the Mediterranean. (Captain Murray Paterson)*

in helping the ship to conform to new rules they effectively mean a new lease of life.

For the conventional vessels, a return to Larne was at one time considered and to that end several visits were made in order to do berthing trials. I had the privilege of taking the *Stena Caledonia* into that once familiar territory on 18th May 2000 on what was the first visit by a Company vessel since 1995. While alongside word came for one of our Second Officers (who lived in the town) that his wife was about to give birth and so our visit did serve one useful purpose though we never did return to commercial service there.

Soon after the *Stena Galloway* returned from a spell of relief work on the Fishguard - Rosslare route towards the end of 2001, an announcement was made that she would be withdrawn at the end of February 2002. By this time I was Senior Master on the *Stena Caledonia* and shared the feeling of sadness felt by all staff that we were to lose our running mate. February 22nd 2002 was a pretty foul day on the North Channel and the 'Galloway' could hardly have picked a worse one for her final sailing on the route. Consequently she was much delayed getting into Belfast and had a small tug standing by to assist. The *Stena Caledonia* was in Harland & Wolff's large drydock for

RECALLING THE 'SAINTS'

*The **Stena Caledonia** is dressed overall in this view whilst participating in the Tour de France. The **Stena Sea Lynx I** can be seen at her berth at Rosslare pending her evening departure to Pembrokeshire. (Gordon Hislip)*

annual refit at this time and a goodly number of us took time out to wistfully watch the end of an era in our lives.

Moroccan interests had bought the 'Galloway' and soon the red ensign was replaced by the red flag of Morocco while at both ends of the ship the name *Le Rif* was very crudely painted on adjacent to where *Stena Galloway* had been obliterated.

Late the following afternoon, the *Le Rif* slipped from the Belfast linkspan for the last time and made her way past the yard where she had been built. The *Galloway Princess* had been Harland & Wolff's newbuilding No. 1713 and it was at 17.13 on 23rd February that she passed her birthplace outward bound for Vigo (for bunkers) and then on to Cadiz where she would be prepared for her new career on the Gibraltar Strait. Nostalgia laden good wishes were conveyed over the V.H.F. then we watched as she made her way out of Belfast beneath two plumes of funnel smoke which had been her lifelong characteristic.

My long-time friend and colleague Captain Robin White was the 'Galloway's' final Stena Master and he with a few others remained onboard for the delivery run. At Cadiz the 'Galloway'/*Le Rif* was joined at the quay by the former *Stena Antrim*.

And so we are one!

The 'Saint' class ships were great servants to Sealink and their successors and a great credit to their designers. That all continue to give valiant service, albeit three of them now doing it for foreign owners in warmer climes, is testimony enough. The *Stena Caledonia* is now the last of the group still doing the kind of job she was intended for and is the final cross-Channel ship built for BR/ Sealink still in service on the U.K. coast. Given a fair breeze she should have plenty of good service still to give.

Those of us who have had a connection with these four vessels over the years have nothing but praise for them. With the passage of time many things cool down, but seldom memories, and in common with many colleagues past and present in all departments, mine remain warm.

J.M. Paterson
Senior Master, *Stena Caledonia*
April 2006

The Saints go marching on

Richard Seville follows the progress of the first three 'Saint' class ships in the western Mediterranean

GALLOWAY PRINCESS/STENA GALLOWAY

2002

The *Stena Galloway* was sold in January to IMTC (International Maritime Transport Corporation) of Morocco, who renamed her *Le Rif* to bolster their fleet on the link between Algeciras and Tangier. No less than six other operators serve this route, but operations were co-ordinated through a pool – which included her half-sister, the former *St Christopher*, as Limadet's *Ibn Batouta*. The former *Stena Galloway* was pressed into service with remarkably few modifications – the only significant change being the conversion of the children's soft play area into a mosque. During her first season in service, many disposables remained onboard, including Stena Line menus in the former Globetrotter Self-Service and even Stena Line branded sugar sachets in the forward bar.

2005

The pool operation in place on the Algeciras to Tangier route was ruled illegal by the EU competition authorities. IMTC now complete independently on the crossing with the *Le Rif* and fleetmate the

The **Le Rif** *(ex* **Galloway Princess***) is little altered from her days at Stranraer. The Moroccan-registered vessel is pictured here off the Spanish coast inward bound to Algeciras. (FotoFlite)*

Atlas, the former *Svea Scarlett* of 1974. Special dispensation has been given for seasonal pool operations from June through to September, however, to ensure the smooth running of the annual 'Operacion Paso del Estrecho', the transportation plan to serve the intense seasonal migration of North African workers to and from Europe. The *Le Rif* remains essentially unchanged from her final years with Stena Line.

ST. ANSELM/STENA CAMBRIA

1999

Following her acquisition by Umafisa, the *Stena Cambria* was

SAINTS IN NEW WATERS

*The **Isla de Botafoc** at Ibiza Town in her final season in Umafisa colours in August 2003. (Richard Seville)*

renamed as the *Isla de Botafoc* and spent nearly a year being prepared for service in Gijon. Spanish sources report the ship was in notably poor condition overall, and the upper vehicle deck ramps even had to be entirely replaced. Umafisa were a local Ibizan operator, whose origins lay in the short route from Ibiza Town to the nearby island of Formentera. The vessel was purchased to launch a new Ibiza Town to Barcelona route; a 9-hour sailing normally completed overnight. It is unsurprising therefore that the changes onboard are extensive - built for a 90 minute crossing, she was effectively converted into an overnight ship and was also given a distinctly Spanish flavour, with local artwork and all her facilities given local names. The main passenger decks, Decks 7 and 8, were renamed Mediterraneo and Atlantico respectively.

Intriguingly, identically to her sister, neither the forward bar nor the self-service cafeteria were significantly altered - both retaining the structure and trim installed in 1986 and 1987/88 respectively right until 2005. Under Umafisa, the forward bar was renamed – bizarrely - the Cafeteria Ibiza. In the forward lobby, however, the bank / bureau de change was converted into a small walk-around shop, whilst the forward starboard side seating area in the cafeteria was enclosed to create a baggage room. The ro-ro drivers' lounge was stripped out and filled with reclining seats to provide overnight sleeping accommodation, and it was designated VIP Salon Cataluna. This space has actually been extended by slightly rearranging the bulkhead positioning between the lounge and the cafeteria seating area. Interestingly, the former door to the Club Class Lounge has been re-located here, complete with the embossed C logo! New local murals were installed in the information area, aft of which all the saloons were replaced with cabins, so the side lounges, games zone, shopping complex and Club Lounge have all disappeared. Small

*The **Isla de Botafoc** entering Barcelona harbour in August 2005. (Richard Seville)*

windows have again appeared in the extension as a result. Moving up to the Promenade Deck, the Globetrotter Restaurant - now the Salon Atlantico was however utterly unchanged under Umafisa. Complete with full Stena Line trim, upholstery, carpeting and even a large Globetrotter mural, it appeared rarely opened to the public. Astern, the Harbour Coffee Co had also become a recliner lounge, Salon Barcelona, and the servery had been enclosed and converted into a baggage room - although inside, all the servery fittings - including sinks and cupboards - remained in place, whilst the HCC branding and artwork remained prominent. Down on A Deck, the former children's play area created from cabin space became an additional recliner lounge, named Salon Formentera. Externally, a small deck bar was installed aft, within the former reserved Motorists' Lounge sun deck. In addition to the new cabins installed, former crew cabins on either side of the vehicle decks were also opened up for passenger use, giving her a total of 78 cabins and 250 berths.

The *Isla de Botafoc* commenced service on her new route in November 1999. Operations were soon pooled with Trasmediterranea who compete on the same route, with interchangeable tickets available. Crossings were operated exclusively overnight, with only a

SAINTS IN NEW WATERS

*The **Isla de Botafoc's** amidships arcade still showing very much evidence of her Sealink British Ferries era. (Richard Seville)*

The premium Sirena-class recliner lounge housed in the former drivers' restaurant. (Richard Seville)

handful of daytime sailings undertaken in peak season.

2003

In August 2003, Umafisa was taken over by rivals Balearia, and services were quickly absorbed into their own network. For the *Isla de Botafoc*, this meant the end of co-operation with Trasmediterranea, repainting in Balearia colours and occasional relief deployment on other Balearic routes. Despite initial predictions that she could be replaced by fast-craft, she continued to play an essential role in the fleet.

2005

As confirmation of her long-term place in the Balearia fleet, prior to the 2005 season, the *Isla de Botafoc* underwent major refurbishment to bring her up to Balearia's own standards. Although her facilities retain their essential functions, all were significantly upgraded with new fittings, upholstery and laminate floorings. The forward Cafeteria Ibiza still remains recognisable as Sealink's traditional British pub, but it has been considerably brightened up and looks extremely attractive. Elsewhere, all her reclining seats were replaced with new premium chairs as are standard throughout the fleet and the Salon Atlantico was converted into a further recliner lounge. Minor changes also included the conversion of the shop forward on Mediterraneo Deck into a new children's play-area and the removal of the baggage store adjacent to the cafeteria servery to re-instate further seating. The VIP Salon Cataluna was also renamed as the Salon Neptuno, presumably for political reasons.

Early in the 2005 season, the *Isla de Botafoc* suffered severe mechanical issues, necessitating the replacement of one of her main engines. She was laid up in Gandia, Valencia, for over two months before returning to service in July 2005. Under Balearia she is utilised far more intensively and for the 2005 season, she operated five times weekly on her original Barcelona to Ibiza Town (Ibiza) route and twice weekly from Barcelona to Mahon (Minorca), sailing out from the mainland overnight and returning during the day. From June she was joined on the Mahon route by her former Sealink and Holyhead fleetmate *Stena Sea Lynx II*, when the latter was chartered in as the *Jaume 1*. Her Ibizan terminal was switched to the newly opened maritime station at San Antonio from July.

ST. CHRISTOPHER/STENA ANTRIM

1998

The *Stena Antrim* was sold in June to Limadet, an established Moroccan shipping company, for service on the Algeciras to Tangier crossing. Her acquisition at first appeared strange, for the company had commissioned a purpose built vessel, the *Ibn Batouta 2*, only five years previously, which the *Stena Antrim* replaced. However, although significantly older than the *Ibn Batouta 2* and highly similar in passenger capacity, the *Stena Antrim* did bring a notable increase in freight capacity, with her internal ramps permitting full use of her twin decks despite limited infrastructure at both ports. No significant changes were made onboard the former *St Christopher*. Operations on the link were run as a pool with other local operators.

2002

Rivals IMTC introduced the *Le Rif* onto the Algeciras to Tangier crossing, the *Ibn Batouta's* half-sister *Galloway Princess*. After initial refusal, IMTC were permitted to join the pool on the route.

2003

Limadet, in precarious financial condition, were taken over by state-run Comanav in late 2003, but continued to trade as a separate entity.

2005

As the *Ibn Batouta*, the former *St Christopher* remains today the flagship of the Limadet operation on the 2 1/2 hour crossing. The pooling agreement on the Algeciras to Tangier crossing, which all six local operators participated in, was ruled illegal by the EU competition authorities in early 2005, but seasonal pool operations continue between June and September under special dispensation to ensure smooth running of the annual 'Operacion Paso del Estrecho' migrations. After seven years Moroccan service, many areas remain instantly recognisable onboard the *Ibn Batouta*. Although re-upholstered, the forward bar and amidships cafeteria are both structurally unaltered from their time as Sealink British Ferries' pub and the Pantry. The bank / bureau de change in the forward lobby is simply closed, whilst the information desk aft in the cafeteria still performs its original purpose. Moving astern, the twin side lounges remain, but the central games zone has been converted into a mosque. Surreally, this space still retains all its Stena Line 'Video Warp' branding and neon trim! The Boat Deck extension is underused, with

SAINTS IN NEW WATERS

*The former **St. Christopher** is seen here at Tangier during her second season on the Gibraltar Straits as the **Ibn Batouta**. (Miles Cowsill)*

much void space - it has been divided into two stores, storage areas and a circulation area. Up on the Promenade Deck, the original tea bar and later bistro has been attractively refurbished to create a VIP / First Class cafe, as is standard on Moroccan vessels. These are not open to the public, but instead are only rarely used for company or even Royal events. The former Motorists' Lounge aft is designated as the VIP / First Class Lounge, but this is currently in notably poor condition, un-refurbished and with many worn and stained fittings. The one-time business-class lounge forward on A Deck is now out of public use. Throughout the vessel, many signs and logos remained from both Sealink and Stena Line.